DEMYSTIFYING DIVERSITY

EMBRACING OUR SHARED HUMANITY

DARALYSE LYONS

FOREWORD BY KYLE V. HILLER

Loving Healing Press

Ann Arbor, MI

Foreword by Kyle V. Hiller

ISBN 978-1-61599-533-2 paperback
ISBN 978-1-61599-534-9 hardcover
ISBN 978-1-61599-535-6 eBook

Library of Congress Cataloging-in-Publication Data

Names: Lyons, Daralyse, author.
Title: Demystifying diversity : embracing our shared humanity / Daralyse
    Lyons ; foreword by Kyle V. Hiller.
Description: Ann Arbor, MI : Loving Healing Press, [2020] | Includes
    bibliographical references and index. | Summary: "Biracial journalist
    Daralyse Lyons interviews more than 100 individuals-academics,
    politicians, thought-leaders, advocates, activists and reveals her most
    important information and insights about diversity, racism, and
    anti-racism. Areas of exploration include the following cultural,
    ethnic, and gender perspectives: biracial, black, and white Americans,
    Latinx, neuro-diverse, LGBTQIA+, body image/types, Holocaust survivors,
    Muslims and Islamophobia, mixed-race couples, and others"-- Provided by
    publisher.
Identifiers: LCCN 2020040251 (print) | LCCN 2020040252 (ebook) | ISBN
    9781615995332 (paperback) | ISBN 9781615995349 (hardcover) | ISBN
    9781615995356 (kindle edition) | ISBN 9781615995356 (epub)
Subjects: LCSH: Multiculturalism--United States. | Ethnicity--United
    States. | Minorities--United States. | Racism--United States. |
    Discrimination--United States. | Toleration--United States.
Classification: LCC E184.A1 .L955 2020 (print) | LCC E184.A1 (ebook) |
    DDC 305.800973--dc23
LC record available at https://lccn.loc.gov/2020040251
LC ebook record available at https://lccn.loc.gov/2020040252

Published by
Loving Healing Press
5145 Pontiac Trail
Ann Arbor, MI 48105

www.LHPress.com   Tollfree 888-761-6268
info@LHPress.com   Fax 734-663-6861

To my mother, Sunny Taylor,
who taught me the value of embracing
myself and others exactly as we are.

Contents

Foreword

I didn't know what code switching was until, in 2016, I discovered NPR's *Code Switch* podcast. I hadn't the vocabulary to articulate something that was happening to me deep down inside: I was having an identity crisis and had been since I was a kid. I grew up in West Philadelphia in a homogenously Black neighborhood. At first, the only White people I ever encountered were my teachers, but there were plenty on TV. For whatever it's worth, I saw as many Black people on TV as I saw White people in real life. That shifted in high school—the school was more diverse. But when I hit college, I was in a sea of White.

What did my elementary, secondary and post-secondary educations all have in common? I felt out of place in each environment, regardless of the shifts. For me, diversity was tumultuous, because I didn't have a strong sense of my place in the world. Of course, I was young, but the microaggressions nestled into the corners of my mind, and I entered adulthood with a contorted sense of self. And I didn't even recognize it until a few years ago, when a few tone-deaf comments from co-workers at a restaurant job made me realize I'd been compromising myself for the sake of others merely to survive. To be me wasn't to thrive—it was a risk.

I was the egghead growing up. I wasn't quite Carlton Banks egghead (maybe somewhere in the awkward middle of Carlton and Will—I was the cool, quiet nerd that everyone liked but didn't really try to get to know), but I did get maligned for my "intelligence." I didn't get bullied in the way we imagine the smart kid in class gets bullied. In fact, my interactions with other students were pretty mild. That, actually, was the problem. No one tried to relate to me, to understand me. They hovered around for one characteristic, scooped it up and ran with it. I grew up with a fear of sharing parts of myself because it was often met with backlash. I got comments like "you're so White" from my Black peers, and my White peers reinforced it with "you're the whitest Black person I know." All because they found out I liked that one Celine Dion CD that Babyface produced? Or that I had diction that they qualified as "talking White?" I was caught in the identity crossroads, fighting to show how I'm just as Black as anyone, and that blasting Carly Rae Jepsen when I need an upbeat bop doesn't detract from that.

But really, can I be so mad at them? They were as young and dumb as me. Unfortunately, it continued well into my adulthood and is more pronounced now than it was then. Luckily, I have more tools to deal with it. This is where *Demystifying Diversity: Embracing Our Shared Humanity* comes in.

Diversity is an uncomfortable term for me. It's something slung most often by White folks, many of whom are just now learning about the disparities afflicting marginalized people. I'm not upset at them for it, but it is exhausting seeing it unfold in real time. It's troubling when I hear people clamoring for diversity when those same people are quick to subvert my identity with comments that are supposed to be in friendly jest. Reading, and editing, Daralyse's book has been an abundant source of clarity, hope and help.

I've got diversity in my family. There are Native Americans in my extended family. I've got family that hails from Puerto Rico and have settled in eastern Pennsylvania, Virginia Beach and southern California. I've got cousins that are as Irish and blue-eyed as the next White person. There's probably more White in our blood than we may know, considering my family was brought here as slaves. I celebrate the diversity in my family, and I honor it with my loved ones outside of those circles. But I don't have to prove that to you, and the diversity in my family doesn't make me any more or less Black. It makes me more diverse, inclusive, empathetic and understanding—virtues I don't think many Americans uphold.

Demystifying Diversity: Embracing Our Shared Humanity is a step forward in mitigating that. Daralyse has comprised an indelible collection of stories and information that casts a wide, embracing light on the unique experiences of many different voices. This book and its companion podcast are the sort of guides I wished existed when I was coming up as a perennial misfit. I think we take for granted how much information has become available to us in the Internet age—which only came out of its infancy in the last ten years. I also think we take for granted how much opportunity for connection the Internet has afforded us. There have been countless relationships I've encountered, and been able to cultivate, that fit and elevate me (and ultimately, each other) because of the Internet: people who look like me, have similar experiences, share the same values and have similar interests. I yearned for books like this, but I didn't know I was yearning. I didn't know I was suffering. I didn't know I was muted because of my "otherness." I didn't know that the complexity of my personality was, in a way, a thing largely because of my curiosity of other cultures—a direct response to my feelings of not belonging. I didn't know so much about my own culture. I didn't know other people were feeling this, and that there was a vast conversation happening around it.

Read this book. Listen to the associated podcast. Share it. Tell your friends. Do the work. Question your biases. Question your identity. We all need to, and *Demystifying Diversity: Embracing Our Shared Humanity* is an important step in our collective, arduous, complex journey towards inclusivity.

Preface

"Without a willingness to confront the human capacity
for hatred, we ensure that persecution and dehumanization will continue"

Daralyse Lyons, author and co-creator of
the *Demystifying Diversity Podcast*

I was at the Boys & Girls Club's after school program, hanging out on
the grass by the side of the building, when I overheard a White girl call
a Black boy the N-word.

I stormed over to where they were standing. "Did you hear what she
called you?"

The boy hung his baseball-capped head.

"Well... What are you gonna do about it?" I wasn't trying to further
intimidate a victim, but I couldn't let the girl get away with hate speech.
I was an eleven-year-old advocate for justice.

Nicole.

I turned to face her.

Nicole went to Western Middle School, like me. We were in the
same grade. She was considerably shorter. The boy must've gone to
Eastern or Central, one of the other two Greenwich Middle schools
because he and I didn't know each other. And Greenwich was the sort
of town where kids of color who went to the same school knew each
other. There were so few of us. Unfortunately, due to what ensued, the
boy and I would never have the opportunity to be formally introduced.

Nicole elongated herself to her full four-feet, three-inches and
planted her hands on her nonexistent hips. She had stringy, mousy-
brown hair that dangled to her shoulders, a pinched face—like a
Doberman's—and beady blue eyes. "Yeah." She sneered. "What're you
gonna do about it, *nigger*?"

The brim of the boy's hat remained pointed at the ground.
"Nothing. I can't hit a girl."

I knew that, if I wanted to remain on the right side of justice, I
couldn't stay a bystander.

"Maybe you can't, but I can!" I delivered an unexpected fist to the gut.

(To this day, that punch remains the only one I've ever thrown—unless you count my brief stint with Billy Blanks Tae-Bo videos, or the six weeks I spent taking Wing Chun lessons).

Before she could react, I leapt on top of her, slapping, clawing, and pulling while she attempted to get away. "Stop! Ow! That hurts! HELP!"

She was crying out, yet she had been the one to inflict the more painful injury.

"You racist pig!" I screamed.

It took three teenage staff members to pull me off and drag me inside to the Program Director's office.

The Program Director, Don, was tall and kind with soft, chestnut eyes and lips that smiled far more often than they frowned. After I told him my side of the story, he sat for several seconds, unmoving. It was as if he wanted to react one way, but knew he had to respond another. What seemed like minutes (but was probably only seconds) later, he instructed me to sit on the bench in the hall outside his office while he called my mom at work.

The hallway was brightly lit and cheery, adorned with children's finger paintings. I stared at a red handprint on yellow construction paper. I didn't quite know how to feel. I wasn't sorry, but I that didn't mean I welcomed whatever punishment awaited.

Mom arrived ten minutes later (two hours before the scheduled dismissal time) to find me still sitting in the hall. By then, Don had interrogated Nicole. He'd gone outside to question her. He and the other staff must've figured that, if they brought her inside, I'd have finished what I started—after she started what she started.

After speaking with my racist peer, Don had remained outside, so he was there to meet my mom, and give her a quick debriefing before the two of them walked in together.

"Dara..." Mom said.

Don held his office door open. Mom and I preceded him inside. He followed, gently closing the door, shutting out any possibility of interruption or intrusion.

"What's this about you calling a girl a racist word?" Mom's expression telegraphed her confusion.

"I didn't call her a racist word."

Don looked from me and my burnished skin to my ivory-complected mother, then back to me again. "Nicole said you did."

"Nicole's a liar!"

"What'd she say Dara called her?" Mom wanted to know.

The Program Director's face flushed as he repeated what Nicole had said I'd said. "White trash."

"Dara! Did you say that?"

"No! I would never say that. You're White. I'm part White. I called her a racist pig."

I explained about Nicole's use of the N-word, and how the boy's unwillingness to hit a girl hadn't precluded me from hitting her on his behalf.

Mom let my version of events sink in. "Oh," she said. And then, "that makes more sense."

"Racism is *wrong*," Don told us both, "and Nicole will be punished. But I can't ignore the fact that Dara assaulted her."

My mom was always a bottom-line-this-for-me person. "So... What's Dara's punishment?"

"She'll be banned from the Boys & Girls Club for the next week."

Mom didn't ask for a partial refund—which was saying a lot considering her tight single-parent budget and her love of bargaining. She thanked the Program Director for his time and told him she appreciated and supported his need to take action. Then, she took my hand and led me outside, to her gold Honda. The car was the same color as my skin in the summer.

"Are you mad?" I asked after we'd climbed inside.

"Not at all," she replied. "Dara, I am super proud of you."

In the twenty-six years since being sent home from the Boys & Girls Club, I've continued to be an advocate for justice, but my approach has changed. I've come to the conclusion that I want to make more of an impact than a punch. Although I believe there's a time and place for violence, I don't think the systems that perpetuate prejudice can be dismantled without engaging with others in meaningful and empathetic ways.

As a Biracial[1] person, I exist in the center of the binaries of Blackness and Whiteness and I hate that so many other people can't seem to embrace both races simultaneously. I'm doing what I can to change that. In 2018, I published a children's book about loving my Biracial identity and, in 2019, I was interviewed on "Community Voices," a local cable TV show, about my understanding of race. The woman who interviewed me, AnnaMarie Jones, is Biracial, like me. She loved my message of acceptance and empowerment and we became immediate friends. We'd each been longing to meet someone with a similar spectrum understanding of race. Not long after our

---

[1] Although most publications do not capitalize the word Biracial, I have elected to do so. It is now standard practice to capitalize races as proper nouns and because I see racial and ethnic identity as existing within a spectrum, it feels important to acknowledge Biraciality as a distinct and separate experience, worthy of the same recognition as any other racial affiliation or identity.

"Community Voices" interview, AnnaMarie called to ask if I wanted to work on a project together.

Her initial idea had been to center our project around anti-racism advocacy, but I wanted to create something more expansive and inclusive.

"I'm in!" I said. "But only if we can find a way to amplify as many marginalized voices as possible."

And, just like that, the *Demystifying Diversity Podcast* was born. I interviewed over 100 individuals and collected more than 100 hours of audio.

There are a lot of -isms and -phobias that go beyond racism and I want to be part of a movement towards equity and inclusion for every human, not just people with whom I share the same racial lineage. Whoever you are, you've likely witnessed, participated in, or been the victim of some form of discriminatory behavior. It might've had to do with race, body shape, gender, religion, or any of the many identity markers that people use to justify their mistreatment of one another.

Through independent research, listening to others, and my own personal experiences, I've become all too aware of the devasting impact of othering (classifying an individual or group of individuals as fundamentally different from one's self). I've come to believe that the only way to overcome dehumanization is to become aware that we all have complex and intersecting identities, to acknowledge the unique gifts that arise from our differences, and to embrace our shared humanity.

I've come to believe that we affect ourselves and each other in three ways:

1. We help.

2. We hurt.

3. We do nothing, remaining un-invested and indifferent.

To help can take a number of forms but any positive contribution requires engagement and empathy. To hurt is also active. It necessitates that we become agents of aggression and dehumanization. Doing nothing is also a form of hurt, but I wanted to create a distinction between active and passive perpetration. By no means does this excuse inaction. On the contrary! It is often those who do nothing who know better and could affect positive change, if only they would be willing to step into the ally zone.

One of my interviews was with Alisa Kraut, Assistant Curator at the National Museum of American Jewish History. The granddaughter of Holocaust survivors, Alisa's father was born in a displaced persons' camp. Unsurprisingly, she had a lot to say about the importance of being invested in the lives, and therefore the deaths, of strangers. She told me that, as human beings, "We're Venn diagrams in Venn diagrams. And so, if you can't find those connections, it means you're not looking."

If you're a human being in this world, you have areas of overlap with people you imagine to be different than yourself. The more we start looking for similarities, the more invested we become. Suddenly, strangers are no longer strange. They are just another iteration of ourselves.

I'm not saying we need to sit around singing Kumbaya, or that we're all one. I'm simply pointing out that discrimination thrives on separation. At the same time, when it comes to the issue of othering, none of us are blameless.

Dr. Howard Stevenson, Constance Clayton Professor of Urban Education and Executive Director of the Racial Empowerment Collaborative, said something that I continue to find useful as I search for commonalities and connections between those of whom I might initially have been suspicious: "the reality is, we can sometimes be initiators ourselves, so you can be both initiator and 'victim.'"

It is not possible to be a human in this world without sometimes displaying the ignorance that lurks on the other side of understanding. Yet, this feels like an especially divisive time to be alive. Especially in America. Since the 2016 election, othering has become so pervasive that it's no longer surprising. The nation's 45th president has been driving a lot of this discrimination and, when he hasn't been instigating it, he's been encouraging and supporting it.

Trump has admitted to grabbing women "by the pussy," mocked a reporter with disabilities, heckled a 12-year-old boy with cerebral palsy, pledged to ban all Muslims from entering the United States, declared that Mexican immigrants are criminals and advocated "building a wall to keep them out," refused to condemn White supremacists, condoned the beating of Black Lives Matter protestors and a homeless Latinx man, stereotyped Jews, made disparaging comments about women based on age and weight, and treated minorities as monoliths—making comments about "the Blacks," "the Mexicans," "the gays," "the Muslims," and "the Hispanics."

To enumerate each of Trump's abuses would be a book in and of itself. (And many such books exist.) Trump didn't create discrimination. He merely stoked the flames of a preexisting fire.

Sadly, America is not the land of freedom, liberty, and individual agency it purports to be. Salaah Muhammad, activist, podcaster, and disruptor, referred to slavery as "the original sin" of our country. I would label it the second sin, after the systematic annihilation of indigenous people. This nation began with the near eradication of Native Americans and indigenous peoples then quickly moved into a nearly 400-year long era of the enslavement of those who happened to have been born Black or Brown.

One of the reasons raced-based persecution has been so pervasive in America and elsewhere is that it capitalizes on visible difference, but early Americans did not confine themselves to persecuting people of color. Just look at the Salem Witch Trials and you'll see how those who came to this country wanting to escape religious persecution morphed from victims to victimizers in an all-too-common manifestation, a manifestation which occurs culturally, societally, and individually.

In her February 2010 publication, "The 'Monster' in All of Us: When Victims Become Perpetrators," feminist, defense attorney, and law professor, Abbe Smith writes:

> Although victims do not always become perpetrators, a truism repeated by prosecutors at sentencing as if it were a profound revelation never before put into words, it is the rare serious perpetrator who was not also a victim. Of course, there are people who commit crime out of self-indulgence, self-interest, meanness, or madness. But among those who have committed serious crime, it is the rare perpetrator who has not also suffered. It is the rare death row inmate whose life does not read like a case study of extreme deprivation and abuse. It is the rare juvenile incarcerated in an adult prison for rape or murder who has had anything other than the cruelest of childhoods. As a career indigent criminal defense lawyer, I live in the world of victims turned-perpetrators. I am often more surprised by my damaged clients who do not commit serious, violent crimes than by those who do. Some might say that this is strange work for a feminist; I spend my time representing mostly men and boys accused of crime and violence, often against women. But, to me, it is all of a piece.

Smith understands that perpetration leads to pain and pain leads to more perpetration. Trauma is cyclical. Standing for human rights requires us to develop our capacity for empathy and to search out the causes that create conditions of violence and victimization. If we don't intervene in restorative and reparative ways, hurt people are likely to hurt other people.

In order to embrace diversity, it's essential to look at the intersectionality of identity and the interconnected nature of oppression.

Much of the information being released into the world today about diversity and inclusion tends to focus on a specific subgroup. There are books, podcasts, and TV shows about the Black Lives Matter movement, the history of slavery, Islamophobia, the mistreatment of individuals with disabilities, weight-based bullying, and all the other topics I present on the *Demystifying Diversity Podcast* and within these pages. While I am grateful for all of this important work, I want to take a broader perspective. By providing an expansive and inclusive look at the experiences of many (but certainly not all) marginalized members of society, I hope to challenge each of us to not only examine our prejudices but to practice empathy for those we assume to be different than ourselves.

Because knowledge without application almost never makes a tangible impact, this book is accompanied by a workbook that includes chapter-by-chapter exercises. Although the workbook is by no means compulsory reading, I invite you to engage with this work and I promise that, if you do, you will expand your capacity to love others and, invariably, that will enable you to more fully love yourself.

If you have the companion *Demystifying Diversity Workbook*, please turn to the exercises for the Preface and start them. Return to Chapter 1 in this book when you have completed them.

1 Diversity and Me: Early Experiences

"You may be hurting because someone has othered you, yet, whether you were aware of it or not, it's likely that you've othered someone else. With empathy and understanding, we can move beyond fear, suspicion, and discrimination into healing, hope, and love."

Daralyse Lyons, author and co-creator of
the *Demystifying Diversity Podcast*

Smoke started wafting up from the back of my head.

My mom yelped and threw the steaming metal hot comb into the kitchen sink. It rattled around the empty silver basin. It was a good thing there weren't any dishes inside, but we generally ate take-out (straight out of the container or off of paper plates) so unwashed dishes were a rarity.

I reached up and touched the nape of my neck. A chunk of singed golden lamb's wool fell to the floor. Luckily, my hair was so thick entire segments of it could go missing without anyone noticing.

Mom skimmed the instructions. "Oh! I should've let the hot comb cool."

I shook my still-smoking head.

"How about a French braid?" Mom suggested.

It couldn't have been easy for a White suburbanite raising a Biracial child in Greenwich, Connecticut—especially as a single parent—but Sunny Lyons then, Taylor now, never subscribed to other people's expectations. When, at seven months pregnant, she discovered that my dad was cheating, she left him. She taught me, by word and by example, that, if anyone mistreated you, you had the right to stand up for yourself.

Who cared if friends or family (or even the ever-present specter of society) second-guessed her ability as a White woman to raise a half-Black daughter? She never doubted herself. And, if people looked at us when we went out, she'd say, "They're staring because you're unique and beautiful."

When I was six or seven, Mom took me to one of my classmate's birthday parties. Two White girls who looked as if they might be around the same age as me approached us.

The one with the blonde pigtails greeted me not with a standard "hello" or "how are you?" but by asking "Are you Black?"

I smiled. "Half Black, and half White."

"Oh," she replied. "Want to play?"

"Yeah," I agreed.

The three of us skipped away together.

I grew up believing that conversations about race could begin from a space of curiosity and connection and my existence as someone who has always claimed equal affiliation with both my Black and White heritage has offered me an entry into a spectrum of different spaces.

In 2018, I published a children's book about my Biracial identity. I'd already published a wide array of adult titles and I was advised that I should differentiate that work from my kids' books by writing *I'm Mixed!* under a pseudonym. I selected Maggy Williams, an amalgamation of my favorite aunt's first name, and my grandfather's middle name (both of them died before the book came out and I wanted to pay tribute to their importance in my life). After publishing the book, I went to various schools, libraries and organizations to read *I'm Mixed!* and speak about embracing all aspects of ourselves and each other. One of the places I went was the same Boys & Girls Club where I once beat up a White girl for calling a Black boy the N-word.

Don, the former Program Director, still worked there, although he'd been promoted several times. "I was so excited to hear about your book," he said when he saw me. We gave each other a huge hug and, when we pulled apart, he told me "I'm proud of you."

It had all come full-circle for me. Unfortunately, the world hasn't fundamentally changed. I still see examples of prejudice everywhere. Although I'm unlikely to throw any physical punches, I still strive to stand up for others. So many people are in need of empathy, advocacy, and allyship because so many others are so hurtful.

During one of my interviews, Dennis Moritz, Jewish poet and playwright, said something that perfectly encompasses what this project has taught me: "I don't think you can be an honest observer of the human condition without being overwhelmed at times by the cruelty that gets visited on people. It seems to me to be so counter to who we are. We're beautiful. Every one of us is beautiful. There is nothing like a human being in this world that we experience. We are remarkable."

Confronting the human capacity for evil doesn't mean losing sight of the beauty and resilience within each of us. In fact, acknowledging both is the only foundation from which to begin the process of repairing the world.

Kinsukuroi, the ancient Japanese art of repairing broken pottery, is a technique that offers a powerful metaphor for my work as an advocate for rights, justice, equality, diversity and inclusion. The Kinsukuroi artist takes broken objects and puts them back together using adhesive that has been infused with precious metals such as silver, platinum, and gold. By treating breakage as part of the item's ever-evolving process, it's always moving towards beauty while honoring brokenness. With the process that you'll be invited to enter into as you read this book and do the exercises in the suggested workbook, you'll be acknowledging breakage even as you look for areas of adhesion.

There is a passage in *A Return to Love: Reflections on the Principles of A Course in Miracles* by Marianne Williamson that recognizes the internal human struggle and calls us to be better, for ourselves and for others:

> As I interpret the *Course [In Miracles]*, 'our deepest fear is not that we are inadequate. Our deepest fear is that we are powerful beyond measure. It is our light not our darkness that most frightens us.' We ask ourselves, who am I to be brilliant, gorgeous, talented and fabulous? Actually, who are you not to be? You are a child of God. Your playing small does not serve the world. There's nothing enlightened about shrinking so that other people won't feel insecure around you. We were born to make manifest the glory of God that is within us. It's not just in some of us; it's in everyone. And as we let our own light shine, we unconsciously give other people permission to do the same. As we are liberated from our own fear, our presence automatically liberates others.

It's not always easy to walk in our light. It is, however, essential to learn to do if we want to stand for equality, justice, liberty, and love. It's even more essential that we embrace the premise that every other human also has a light within them and none of us are more valuable than any other.

Not every person, or even every demographic, is represented in these pages. Nevertheless, you will find a multitude of different stories and will be able to relate to at least some of the wide-ranging human experiences shared within this book. As you read, and as you work through the accompanying workbook, I urge you to let yourself expand beyond the limits of what you think you know about yourself and others. It's okay to feel broken at times. In fact, I hope you do. It's part of the process and it's within the cracks that you'll find yourself most receptive to the growth that is adhesive—the human connection that is gold.

If you have the companion *Demystifying Diversity Workbook*, please turn to the exercises for Chapter 1 and start them. Return to Chapter 2 in this book when you have completed them.

2 Encountering the Black/White Binary

"Just as deep as the issues of systemic racism are, so should be the lessons to overcome them."

AnnaMarie Jones, co-creator of
the *Demystifying Diversity Podcast*

Other than at the Boys & Girls Club at age eleven, the only other time I heard the N-word was in my late teens. Before transferring to NYU, I attended Molloy College on a volleyball scholarship. By the time I got there, I was a full-blown anorexic and bulimic and struggling with issues that had nothing to do with race but still made me feel isolated and ashamed. My volleyball peers were all rich, White and entitled. We had little to nothing in common.

One evening, while traveling for a pre-season tournament, the fourteen of us were sitting in the hotel lounge, waiting for our head and assistant coaches to get back from Subway with everybody's food and talking about boys, parents, school, and our goals for the future.

"My goal is to get my dad to buy me a Mustang for my birthday," Tara, the team's back-up setter, declared. She explained that getting a car gift counted as a goal because she had a clear, linear plan of acquisition, including begging and manipulation. (Side note: Midway through the season, her dad did buy her the brand-new white Mustang, so I guess that was an achievement).

Somehow, the conversation drifted to pet peeves and, Alicia, a freshman, and that year's right-side-hitter, posed a question to the group "You know who I hate?"

We all turned to face her.

"No," Ashley replied. "Who?"

"Niggers."

I took a deep breath. The rest of my teammates remained blank-faced. They weren't going to say or do anything. It was up to me to take a stand, not only for one half of my race, but for what was right.

"You know…" Although I kept my eyes locked on Alicia, I could sense the others shifting in their seats. "I'm half Black."

"Oh. Well, of course, I didn't mean *you*." She backpedaled. "I meant *niggers*."

"I'm not familiar with what you mean by that," I replied through gritted teeth. "What, exactly, constitutes a *nigger*?"

She waved a hand dismissively. "You know. An ignorant Black person."

I stood. "I don't know any ignorant Black people, but, evidently, you're an ignorant White one."

When I walked away, no one chased after me. I'm not sure what, if anything, was said in my absence, but, from then on, every time I saw Alicia, I saw ignorance and intolerance. When I looked at our other teammates, I couldn't respect them. The notion of an "innocent" bystander is, in practice, more often mythology than reality.

Eventually, I transferred to NYU. Living in a diverse city, surrounded by people from all backgrounds, I felt a sense of belonging. Not that there wasn't intolerance in New York. Prejudice is everywhere, and not all prejudice comes from White people. I learned this years ago.

When I was nine, Mom took me to Brooklyn to visit our African homeopath—the one who cured me of seizures with a single dose of a homeopathic remedy. While I was in his office talking about rubrics and repertoires, she sat in the waiting room leafing through a copy of *Ebony Magazine*.

A striking African American woman walked in.

Mom perked up. "Hi!"

Mom always enjoys talking to strangers. Take her anywhere where random people congregate—cafeteria-style restaurants, airports, the grocery store, banks, and hotel lobbies—and she'll leave knowing at least three individual's life stories.

The stranger sported dreadlocks that hung to the small of her back and a tiny gold ring in her left nostril. She looked the woman who'd birthed me up and down, then took a seat in the opposite corner of the room.

Mom didn't take the hint. "Isn't Dr. Kokayi wonderful? How long have you been seeing him?"

Nose Ring selected something of her own from the available-reading stack: *Callaloo: A Journal of African Diaspora Arts and Letters*.

"He's helped my daughter so much. We don't even live in Brooklyn, but we drive two round-trip hours every month because he's a genius. Is this your first time here?"

Nose Ring rolled her eyes at the chocolate-skinned receptionist behind the counter, as if to say *Can you believe this White Lady has the audacity to try to talk to me?*

"I prefer to keep to myself," the stranger said.

"Okay." Mom went back to perusing her black-is-beautiful magazine.

A few minutes later, when I emerged from the doctor's inner sanctum, she wasn't in the lobby. She'd gone down the hall to the bathroom.

A gorgeous woman in flowing white robes with a gleaming nose ring and rows of long, thin dreadlocks smiled at me from behind her glossy-covered *Callaloo*. "Why hello."

I returned her grin. "Hi! You here for Dr. Kokayi?"

"Yes. Isn't he wonderful?"

"Yeah. He's helping me with my asthma."

"Asthma? A beautiful girl like you shouldn't suffer with asthma..."

Mom walked back in. I handed her a blue, Boiron tube. "Dr. Kokayi gave me a new remedy!" I declared.

"That's great, Dara." She squinted at the tiny vial. She needed glasses but was too self-sacrificing to buy herself a pair. "What is it?"

The stranger looked startled. "*This* is your mother?"

Mom stuck out her hand. "Nice to meet you. I'm Sunny. What's your name?"

Nose Ring reluctantly allowed Mom's pink-fleshed fingers to grasp her mahogany ones. "Imani Utawala is what I've christened myself following my emancipation from the systematic oppression of my people by the White man."

The lady at the desk shuffled through her folders. I was pretty sure that, for insurance purposes, she knew Imani Utawala as Wanda, Lisa, or Elizabeth, with some standard surname, like Jones. (When we got home, Mom and I looked up the meaning of the stranger's self-assigned names.)

Still, the knowledge that Mom had once engaged in jungle-fever love made Faith and Domination soften enough that her daggers were downgraded to those Nerf swords my cousin Kelvin played with. Still capable of inflicting pain. Not sharp enough to cut.

When the two of us were in her gold Honda, heading back to Greenwich, my remedy tucked into her purse, to be taken later—an hour away from food—Mom told me about what had transpired before I emerged from Dr. Kokayi's office. "That woman wouldn't give me the time of day until she knew I was with you. Even then, she wasn't exactly effusive."

"I know," I agreed. "She was nice to me. Why would she treat us differently?"

"I'm pretty sure it's a race thing."

"Race is just the color of your skin. It shouldn't matter."

"It shouldn't. Unfortunately, for some people, it does."

I think that we are doing each other and ourselves a massive disservice by treating Black and White as two opposing, binary forces. I also think we're doing a disservice by acknowledging that there is a spectrum of Blackness while refusing to accept that, if that's true, there's also a spectrum of Whiteness.

When I refer to a "spectrum of Blackness," I'm referring to the fact that, as disturbing as it is, there are a slew of YouTube videos, memes, GIFs and jokes depicting various stereotypical attitudinal differences between lighter and darker skinned people of color. While this is egregious and insensitive, it speaks to the fact that within conceptions of Blackness there is a sense that there is not uniformity. We see evidence of colorism operating all the time and Black people speaking about the skin-privilege of their lighter-skinned Black and Biracial counterparts.

Whiteness is different. The cultural conversation around White identity presents this particular race as an absolute and a binary. Whereas Blackness has shades and a spectrum, when it comes to Whiteness, one either is or one isn't. That's not to say that there are never instances of binary Blackness, and that those can't be perpetrated by both Black and White people, but there does seem to be an overwhelming sense that Blackness and Whiteness are mutually exclusive.

Jose Gonzales, Director of Graduate Support at GESU School, a dedicated anti-racist and a Biracial Polish and Puerto Rican man, informed me "The more people we can get in that dialogue getting comfortable with their Whiteness and understanding the history of Whiteness in America and the world, the more we can start having authentic conversations about race and not only saying 'I'm not racist,' but offering anti-racist content, anti-racist advocacy, anti-racism language. It's not okay to just say, 'I'm not racist.' Okay, that's great, but are you anti-racist?"

I would argue that being anti-racist means refusing to perpetrate antiquated notions of race that can be traced back to slavery and refusing to be constrained by the systems of oppression that support White privilege.

White supremacist Craig Cobb's ancestral lineage was traced back through DNA profiling to reveal that he is 14% Black. I wonder if knowing this early in his life might have prevented some of his hatred towards those with whom he shares at least a fractional connection. By the time he found out his true racial identity, he'd already been so indoctrinated in the philosophy of hate that it was too late to have an impact. He denied who he was. And, as a result of his refusal to see himself, all he could see when he looked at the world continued to be the Black/White binary and his own hatred projected from himself outward onto others.

I have no desire to discount or invalidate the lived experience of any person. However, part of not discounting lived experience necessitates creating space for people to exist in spaces that aren't always easily classifiable. The movement towards a spectrum understanding of gender identity and sexual orientation has a lot to teach us. Hopefully, we would never ask a person with non-binary or two-spirit gender identity, or a person who is bi- or pansexual to "choose a side." I know that this happens all too often (partly because it's happened to me), but due to the tireless activism of the LGBTQIA+[2] community, we are moving towards more flexible understandings of sexuality and gender. It would be great if we could do the same with race.

Even those who consider themselves "woke" don't seem to see a problem with forcing people to adopt definitions that have been codified into culture but are not reflective of their lived experience. My lived experience has included a more spectrum understanding of race and, in the next chapter, I explore the lived experiences of others because there is an entire rainbow between the Black/White binary.

If you have the companion *Demystifying Diversity Workbook*, please turn to the exercises for Chapter 2 and start them. Return to Chapter 3 in this book when you have completed them.

---

[2] LGBTQIA+ encompasses Lesbian, Gay, Bisexual, Pansexual, Transgender, Genderqueer, Queer, Intersexed, Agender, Asexual, and Ally communities.

3 What Biracial Identity Can Teach Us

"It feels like there's something very distinct to the biracial experience where it's like well which side are you closer to? And somehow that gets defined by external appearance as opposed to culture or experience. I remember, growing up, people asking me the question 'Well, you're mixed, but which one are you?' As if I had to pick at age nine or something. I wanted to say, 'It's not and it's never been like that. Being mixed is just a different thing'."

Malcolm Burnley, award-winning multimedia
journalist, contributor to the Fuller Project

I was eight years old, sitting in a breakout room with a group of approximately ten kids of various ages. We were all Biracial, half-Black and half-White, and all part of the same Interracial Couples and Biracial Children's group. We'd been in the room for about ten minutes when the facilitator asked us to go around the room and state our race.

"Black."

"Black."

"Black."

The children before me said.

When it was my turn, I stated, matter-of-factly, "I'm part Black and part White."

"Yeah," the facilitator acknowledged. "But which one are you?"

"What do you mean?"

"I mean which one?"

"I'm not one. I'm two. Biracial—Black and White."

The teacher seemed unsure whether to accept my perspective or challenge it, so she did both. "Okay," she said. "Technically, you're Black and White, but the world sees you as Black."

"Why would I define myself based on how the world sees me?"

"We exist within a society."

"But society gets things wrong all the time. Society is responsible for slavery and lynching and discrimination against women and a million other horrific things. We shouldn't let society change us. We should change society."

The facilitator could tell that I was not going to dispense with my opinion, or my conception of myself, so she shook her head then moved on.

"Black."

"Black."

"Black."

After everyone else had identified, ignoring their White parent who was sitting just a few feet away, in the other room, the facilitator moved on to her intended lecture. She informed our assembled group that, as Black kids, our lives were destined to be harder. I didn't buy into anything she said. How much could she teach me? She claimed to be an expert on race yet couldn't understand the concept of Biraciality.

After she finished, the facilitator left us in our breakout room while she returned to the main room to debrief our parents, half of whom were the color of chocolate, the other half of whom were vanilla.

"Well, all of the children identified as Black except one who is adamant that she is both Black and White."

All the other parents turned towards my mom. In the racial "expert's" absence, the interracial couples had been engaged in an impassioned debate. Everyone else had been adamant: If a person had any amount of fractional Blackness, they needed to claim their Blackness to the exclusion of their Whiteness. Mom had been the only dissenting voice in the room. "Why would I let society dictate how I teach my daughter about race?" she'd asked at the same time as I'd been saying "Why would I let society tell me how to define myself?"

It turns out, the facilitator was correct about societal perceptions, but I was even more correct about the pain engendered by succumbing to the strictures imposed by a society that has been built on prejudice and privilege.

I'm glad I was taught to embrace all aspects of my identity, not just within myself, but also to others. Despite realizing that this expansive way of understanding my race was unusual, I didn't realize how unusual until I began researching the statistics. The overwhelming tendency amongst Black, White and Biracial Americans remains to view Black-White Biracial people as "more Black than White." So much so that Black/White Biracial adults are three times more likely to identify as Black than as White, Biracial, Mixed, or Multiethnic.

This practice of Biracial individuals being culturally codified as Black dates back to slavery and "the one drop rule," wherein if a person possessed so much as one drop of "colored blood," they would be considered Black. This rule was designed with the soul aim of stripping anyone with any Black ancestral lineage of their rights, the most basic of which was freedom.

This isn't to say that this way of classifying Blackness was solely important to White slave-owners. It was also critical to the maintenance of Black culture and the cohesion of Black families. The majority of Biracial children during slavery were conceived when White slave owners forced themselves onto their Black female "property" and, even in the cases when the sex wasn't violent, it wasn't consensual. When you have been designated as someone else's property, you don't have a choice. They can use your body however and whenever they choose.

I'm not saying that Biracial people shouldn't be allowed to claim Blackness to the exclusion of Whiteness. But I don't want past definitions of race, that are rooted in subjugation and oppression, to dictate our present conceptions of who we are and where we fit in the world.

I support anyone's right to identify with whatever race they choose (provided they are, in fact, that race and not trying to pull a Rachel Dolezal), yet I can't help but wonder if some Biracial people who are claiming Blackness to the exclusion of their Whiteness might be doing so based on the racist roots of the one drop rule and, where that's the case, I hope that seeing that self-identification as a perpetration of prejudice will enable them to step outside the existing social strictures. The way to combat systemic racism isn't to fit ourselves into pain-inducing systems. It's to change the systems and the problems they perpetuate.

I had an illuminating conversation with Malcolm Burnley, a Philadelphia-based journalist and the author of the article "My Biracial Life: A Memoir," about how we both see race as a spectrum rather than as binary. "I came to the conclusion that my experience has been much more that of a Mixed person than that of a Black person," he told me. "What I mean by that is that, throughout my life, I've pretty much only been identified as an other, or identified as non-White. That much has been clear. But it's not always been clear that I've been Black. There's a space in between that I've occupied, and the ambiguity of that is an experience in itself that's unique."

Yes! There is something unique about existing within the space between Black and White. Or, at least, there can be.

"The experiences of some people who are Mixed, who look a certain way, maybe it makes more sense for them to identify as Black," Malcolm said. "But there is a whole group of us who are Mixed who I think probably feel like we do, which is that that category is important to our experience and tells something specifically that you could not say if you identify as Black."

In 2015, before she married a prince and temporarily stepped into a modern-day fairytale only to step out again (it's been speculated partially due to racism and othering perpetrated against her by the British royal family and British press), then Meghan Markle, now the Duchess of Sussex, wrote an article for *Elle Magazine*. In it, she writes "To describe something as being [B]lack and [W]hite means it is clearly defined. Yet when your ethnicity is [B]lack and [W]hite, the dichotomy is not that clear. In fact, it creates a grey area. Being [B]iracial paints a blurred line that is equal parts staggering and illuminating... There was a mandatory census I had to complete in my English class—you had to check one of the boxes to indicate your ethnicity: [W]hite, [B]lack, Hispanic or Asian... My teacher told me to check the box for Caucasian[3]. 'Because that's how you look, Meghan,' she said. I put down my pen. Not as an act of defiance, but rather a symptom of my confusion... I didn't tick a box. I left my identity blank—a question mark, an absolute incomplete—much like how I felt... When I went home that night, I told my dad what had happened. He said the words that have always stayed with me: 'If that happens again, you draw your own box.'"

I don't see the space between Black and White as only grey. I see it as a rainbow of colors, a rainbow that exists on the other side of the rainstorm of racism. That's not to say that every Black/White Biracial person needs to self-identify that way, but it does seem that occupying the spectrum space between White and Black comes with its own set of pressures and privileges and that there's no way to meaningfully engage with that reality without acknowledging it.

A Biracial life experience is different than a Black one, or a White one.

I want to be clear: There is no one experience of Blackness and no one experience of Whiteness. There are only individual experiences, and there are as many of those as there are individuals. However, at the same time, there are certain common occurrences that many people who fit within a certain racial classification experience.

Anecdotal evidence and statistics suggest that the majority of Black Americans, especially Black adult males, have experienced race-based discrimination and/or racial profiling, that many members of the Muslim faith who wear a head scarf experienced bone-deep fear after Trump entered the Oval Office, and that a significant percentage of the LGBTQIA+ community has felt shoved back into the closet when they tried to emerge from it.

In my conversations with other Biracial Americans, every single one of us has stories about having been asked to "pick a side."

---

[3] Caucasian is an outdated term that you will not see included elsewhere in this book; however, this is a direct quote and so it remains unaltered.

Isabel Ballester, who, despite being born to a White mother, identifies as either Black or Afro-Latina, told me that the side she picked was Black. She went on to say that "it feels really weird to be White-passing light skinned and to fight to take up space as a person of color. I feel super judged by that. I'm like, but you don't understand what it is like not being Black enough and not being White enough, or being too Black for the White family, too White for the Black family."

In listening to Isabel's experiences, I was struck by how excruciating it can be to feel as if you don't fit in anywhere, especially when my own experience has mostly enabled me to fit in everywhere. Russita Buchanan, whose mom is Black and whose dad is White, told me "One of the things that I think is great about being multiethnic is that, because we look the way that we do, and we have experiences with White people and Black people, we understand some of the nuances of both cultures that other people who come from one culture or one ethnicity wouldn't know. We can kind of just blend in and fit in wherever we go, and we're accepted pretty much most places."

Now that she's an adult, Russita feels as if she belongs, but she hasn't always felt that way. She was called the N-word in middle school and described the experience as "pretty common." For me, it wasn't common. Both times I was exposed to that language, the slur wasn't directed at me, which I believe made it easier to take a stand.

In 2002, I had my Ancestry DNA profile done and discovered that my ancestors are from Nigeria, Mali, Benin and Togo, Cameroon, Ghana, Senegal, Ireland and Scotland, Italy, Eastern Europe, England, and France. Previously, I'd believed that I was African American, Native American, French, Irish and Italian and, although I did find myself wishing for indigenous ancestry, I also felt a deep sense of connection to truth and authenticity. I also felt validated insofar as I'd been claiming my diversity for all of my existence. Others with similar DNA profiles have not. I can't help but wonder if discovering their true ethnic breakdown challenged their self-conception.

As Isabel put it, "I think what's tricky is that the way I go about the world is not a White experience, either because of how people perceive me, or even the way that I experience things, so it's easier for me to say I'm Afro-Latina because that's the closest language I have to naming my experience. But being raised by a White mom as a kid of color is a whole other layer of identity. Like what does it mean to be like Afro-Latina but raised by a White mom? That comes up all the time—all the time—probably at least once a day."

By subsuming Biracial identity into Black identity, without regard to nuance, personal experience, or parentage, we erase the complexity of the actual nature of race relations in favor of quick categories and binary conceptions of something that isn't always binary. We eradicate the particular pain of the souls of Black people and negate the unique anguish that can come from a more ambiguous identity.

Isabel told me "I can occupy White spaces in a safer way than some other Brown people and Black people, but there are a lot of ways in which I am just as at risk strictly based on the fact that I'm mixed and people really have a problem with that. My safety comes into question not necessarily because I'm Black but more so because I am also White… White people respond to me in rude ways, Black people respond to me in a rude way, and mostly it's for the same reason."

The shift towards a more expansive understanding of racial identity would allow us all to embrace more inclusive perspectives of others and of ourselves.

The experience of being Black in America is different than the experience of being Biracial. Those with lighter skin and Whiter features (whatever that means) tend to receive preferential treatment and, therefore, find themselves in the position of greater, if still not quite White, privilege.

Every single one of my Biracial interviewees spoke about how the racism we Black/White Americans experience throughout our lifetimes is often less overt, and less obvious, than the racism that gets visited on our Black siblings. I think it's essential to acknowledge this. Why? Because racism will never be overcome if light-skinned Black and Biracial individuals continue to be granted greater access to privileges while those with darker skin continue to be subjugated, profiled, and persecuted while simultaneously being told that we are "making progress." It's not progress to transition from oppressing all people of color to using skin-privilege and colorism to discriminate against some and elevate others.

According to a 2006 article, "Study: Darker-skinned Black Job Applicants Hit More Obstacles," Matthew Harrison, a doctoral student at UGA, conducted a colorism in hiring study and discovered the following:

> We found that a light-skinned Black male can have only a bachelor's degree and typical work experience and still be preferred over a dark-skinned Black male with an MBA and past managerial positions, simply because expectations of the light-skinned Black male are much higher, and he doesn't appear as 'menacing' as the darker-skinned male applicant.

When we start to really look at who's being granted access and opportunities, we start to see that the conflation of Biraciality and Blackness skews the data and allows mainstream culture to obfuscate responsibility for the pervasive prejudice that darker Black Americans experience.

When we say we've had a Black president or that ABC is hosting their first-ever season with a Black bachelor, we're ignoring that Barak Obama and Matt James are each half White and, as such, we're ignoring that many positions of power and influence continue to be untenable for Black Americans.

In a June 7th, 2020 Instagram post, Matt James referred to White people saying things in reference to his having access to certain spaces such as "It's cool. His mom is [W]hite."

Let's unpack this. James is flat-out saying that, in rampantly racist America, his Whiteness has made his access and advancement less of a "threat" than if he'd been entirely Black. Matt James and former President Obama and so many others are entitled to every scrap of success they've been able to achieve, so I'm not undermining their personal or professional accomplishments. I'm simply making the point that those of us who carry any Whiteness within ourselves would do well to examine our skin-privilege, something we can only do by getting painfully honest about the fact that many more of us than we've been admitting carry within ourselves a simultaneous ancestral legacy of victim and victimizer.

I've always believed that for me to identify with one race to the exclusion of the other would both strip me of an important segment of myself and create a disingenuous impression of my lived reality. To my knowledge, I've never been actively discriminated against due to race or had doors closed because of the color of my skin or texture of my hair, but I didn't fully become aware of my skin-privilege until I went back to Connecticut in 2016 for my fifteen-year high school reunion. While I was there, I met my friend Jay for lunch at Chipotle.

Jay is a dark-skinned Black man, I a medium-complected Biracial woman. We grew up in the same town, attended the same schools, were raised by strong, independent mothers and were friendly throughout all of middle and high school. He'd been well-behaved, personable, kind and industrious whereas I'd been a slacker and a delinquent. (My junior year of high school, I skipped classes on 82 out of 182 school days!)

Until that lunch, I'd assumed that Jay's experiences of race had mirrored mine, but when we started discussing it, I realized I could not have been more wrong.

The supposedly liberal members of our Greenwich High School and Western Middle School classes, their parents and teachers, and the school administrators had treated me as an asset and him as a liability. Jay told me about pejorative comments, being left out of parties, dads forbidding him from dating their daughters, and feeling tokenized by his White friends.

I apologized for not having been a better friend.

He shrugged. "Honestly, Dara, I'm so used to it that it hardly ever has an impact anymore."

For me to claim Blackness to the exclusion of Whiteness would mean that, when speaking about my racial encounters, I would paint a picture of progress and inclusion. I would erroneously say things like "I'm a Black woman and I've had a life full of opportunities for advancement and inclusion. Sure, there might've been a few instances where I was exposed to overt racism, but, by and large, despite systemic problems, most of the individuals I've encountered have been anti-racist and inclusive."

That would be a lie. I have had a life full of opportunities for advancement and inclusion, but not as a Black woman. As a half-White one.

Malcolm Burnley described his Biracial experience as follows: "It's like simultaneously feeling special and separate. It's this weird thing. You feel really lonely despite the fact that you feel like you're being noticed."

When it comes to racial and ethnic identity, I don't pretend to have all the answers, but I do know that the more we encourage one another to acknowledge and embrace all aspects of our identities, the more inclusive society becomes. This doesn't mean ignoring history or the ways that it continues to inform how we think, feel, and behave. On the contrary. It means being brave enough to get honest about the ways in which our present is still being shaped by the past.

When AnnaMarie Jones (my co-collaborator for the *Demystifying Diversity Podcast*) spoke to her White mother about racism, her mom told her "When you don't know something, and you don't understand it, you fear it."

Many White people fear Blackness because they don't know and understand it and many Black people fear Whiteness because they've experienced the negative ramifications of unchecked privilege in action. Those of us who are Biracial are more likely to have positive experiences of both Whiteness and Blackness. This isn't always the case, of course, but, if we've interacted with both our parents, and/or both sides of our family, we'll have at least had some exposure to both sides of the spectrum.

The numbers of multiracial children being born is growing at an exponential rate, three times faster than the U.S. population as a whole. In 1970, one percent of the babies born were multiracial, as compared to ten percent in 2013. As of 2015, multiethnic Americans accounted for 6.9% of the total population. It is estimated that by the year 2045, being Biracial or multiethnic will cease to be the exception. It will be the rule.

If we hope to create a more loving, inclusive society, we need to start being more inclusive in our modes of self-definition.

Today, when I visit schools, libraries, bookstores, organizations and the like to read them my children's book, *I'm Mixed!*, after story time is over, I'll ask the kids about all the things that make them who they are. I listen to their experiences and I learn about the ways in which they are almost always holding simultaneous conceptions of themselves. We'll talk about the color of our skin—I've met chocolate kids and vanilla, caramel and cashew. The kids tell me I'm sand in the winter, honey in the summer. They hardly ever seem to feel a need to define themselves by others' conceptions of who they're supposed to be, and, most of the time, they embrace themselves exactly as they are.

As I think back to the room where, as a child, I was the only voice in ten that self-identified as Biracial, I wish that, instead of lecturing us about the inevitable difficulty of being Black in America, the facilitator had instead spoken to us about the important role we could play, should we choose to accept it.

Whether or not we asked for it, most of my Biracial interviewees reported feeling as if, in their families, they offered a source of unification, love, and connection.

I feel the same. My Biraciality is evidence that, at least for the time it took to conceive me, Blackness and Whiteness came together and created something beautiful. It seems to me that there's a lesson to be gleaned from that. What's more, I don't think it's possible to love and accept people of other races until we can love and accept our own race, or races. This doesn't mean loving the evils that've been perpetrated by our ancestral predecessors. Acknowledging and condemning those evils is important. It's part of reckoning with our own privilege.

Being able to sit in the space of your Whiteness, Blackness, Biraciality, or any other racial or ethnic background, or combination of backgrounds, is essential to understanding that none of us should ever apologize for our race, defend against it, or deny elements of who we are. Instead, we need to embrace the full spectrum of our identity and, from there, learn to love and accept everybody else.

If you have the companion *Demystifying Diversity Workbook*, please turn to the exercises for Chapter 3 and start them. Return to Chapter 4 in this book when you have completed them.

4   **No More Bystanders**

> "The human mind is a complicated theatre of aggression, but also victimization, and all these different feelings interact with each other in very complicated ways that shape who we are."
>
> Steven Weitzman, Director at the Katz Center for
> Advanced Judaic Studies at UPenn

The day after their family store was vandalized, 15-year-old Bill Schwabe and his mother went to see if anything could be salvaged. Bill's body was trembling. Even though the previous night's mob had long-since dissipated, he could hear the sounds of shattering glass and screams.

Kristallnacht (the Night of Broken Glass) had upset whatever fragile equilibrium Bill, his mother, and his five-year-old sister, Eva Ruth had been attempting to maintain since, days earlier, when the family patriarch had been dragged away. Bill's father had been taken by the Schutzstaffel (SS), the major paramilitary organization under Adolf Hitler and the Nazi Party.

Bill's mother had insisted Eva Ruth remain at home while she and Bill went to the store. Not that the little girl didn't know that, as Jews, they were in constant danger, but Mrs. Schwabe wanted her daughter to maintain at least a vestige of her childhood.

Of himself, Bill wrote in his as-yet unpublished memoir, *A Journey Through Separate Worlds: My life from 1923 to the present,* "Adulthood usually comes gradually, as human beings grow physically and experience life. For me, adulthood came suddenly in November 1938."

The vandals had been merciless. The Schwabes' storefront windows were shattered. Clothes were ripped to shreds. Bags of flour had been torn open, their contents spilling out onto the floor. Bill recalled "The store had been completely vandalized. The heavy metal cash register almost barred entrance through the front door. Bolts of cloth had been torn from the shelves and lay helter-skelter inmidst of mounds of broken glass."

Everything valuable had either been stolen or destroyed and left behind, which somehow seemed more menacing. The Germans didn't just want more for themselves; they wanted the Jews to have nothing. Nothing. Did that include taking their lives? Maybe the rumors were true.

Bill stood in the entryway, not wanting to go inside, reluctant to face the evidence of all-pervasive hatred.

The Nazis had his father. If they could do this to a store, imagine what they were doing to him.

When she crouched down to the ground and began picking up pieces of broken glass, Mrs. Schwabe knew that cleaning wouldn't salvage anything worthwhile, yet she needed to do something. Anything. She needed a sense of agency, no matter how small, regardless of the circumstances.

The mother/son pair heard the sounds of footsteps approaching and looked at one another, their eyes wide, their bodies on alert. *Were the looters returning?* No. The figure who appeared was recognizable. She'd been working at the Schwabes' family store for nearly as long as Bill had been alive.

"My father's most loyal employee, Mrs. Pelzer, and my mother began to repair the damage the best they could" Bill would later write. "It was a moment that required the utmost in courage on the part of both women and it was a moment when my mother, who had always been dependent on my father, rose to the occasion. I still see two women struggling on their knees to salvage merchandise, to struggle in righting furniture, to strain in moving the heavy broken cash register away from the door."

In some ways, Bill and his family were among the lucky ones. His father bribed the SS guards into releasing him, and he returned to his family alive. But, for those who experienced the Holocaust, there is no luck. There are only those who died and those who lived but lost something irretrievable.

A 96-year-old Bill told me "When my father thought of the past, he thought of the people that he knew, some of whom made it out and did very well and some of course died and some of them died gruesome deaths, really bad deaths. He never talked about this, but I'm sure that it was never far from his mind."

Bill's family fled Hanau, Germany in 1939 with almost nothing, and the four of them began a new life in a new country. The past continued to have an enduring impact.

The trauma of having been persecuted, beaten, driven out of their home country, losing everything, knowing friends and loved ones (including both grandmothers) had died, and immigrating from a hostile Germany to an unreceptive America had taken their toll, especially on Mrs. Schwabe. "My mother who was very brave during the Nazi period when everything was destroyed became very anxious, so anxious," Bill recounted. "Almost pathological. She worried constantly about nothing and my father's role was to explain that the worries were groundless. But her anxieties stemmed from the experiences that she had."

Bill was not an anxious person. He was optimistic. I spoke with Bill several dozen times and met him three times in person—once at his apartment for our on-the-record interview, once to accompany him on a trip to the National Liberty Museum in Philadelphia and once to meet him and his friend at their assisted living facility for an early-bird dinner.

I noticed something remarkable about Bill. Whenever he spoke about his experiences during the Holocaust, he eventually came back to the story of Ms. Pelzer, the faithful employee who arrived on the morning after Kristallnacht to assist the Jewish family that she knew and loved.

My interviews with Holocaust survivors, their spouses, children, and grandchildren has taught me that there is no such thing as an innocent bystander.

The word bystander means one who is present but not taking part in an event, a spectator. But spectatorship is endorsement. If a watcher is being actively threatened, they may have to wait to intercede, but if you see evil occurring, whether against one individual or on a massive scale, and don't take action to intercede, or assist, you're endorsing dehumanization.

Bystanders were by far the overwhelming majority of people to go through the Holocaust. While their fellow humans were dragged from their homes, taken to death camps, and murdered, there were many who told themselves *It's not my fight. I'm staying out of it.* This obfuscation of responsibility enabled the Nazis to murder more than eleven million people. If more of these bystanders had been upstanders, millions of lives could have been saved.

It is not just individuals who are culpable. It's organizations and even nations. Countries sat on the sidelines, like spectators at a football game, and feigned investment but did nothing to involve themselves and stop the senseless suffering of others. Or they waited far too long and did far too little.

I'm not saying those who witness evil bear the same responsibility as those who perpetrate it. However, it's untrue to claim that passively watching others be harmed is a neutral act. It isn't.

Most modern-day bystander situations are not life or death. There are some, including the fatal stabbings of Ricky John Best and Taliesin Myrddin Namkai-Meche when they attempted to aid a Muslim

American woman during an Islamophobic assault by Jeremy Joseph Christian. But the interventions life requires of you won't be those in which you're risking danger, death, or persecution. Instead, you need to be willing to risk temporary discomfort or inconvenience.

It's difficult to tell a client, friend, or family member "please don't say that" or to report your boss to Human Resources for their discriminatory attitudes towards fellow employees. But, if we want to arrest (and ultimately reverse) the spread of hate, we have to take a stand, not just once but every time we witness injustice in action. You don't have to get this perfectly. In fact, perfection is impossible.

I work with these issues and am constantly thinking about the importance of equality and inclusion and sometimes I'll be at a party or in a group meeting and someone will make an inappropriate joke and I won't even think to say something until after the moment has passed.

Not too long ago, one of my clients made a comment about seeing a large-bodied woman on the beach and being disgusted by her choice of outfit. By the time his remark registered, our conversation had ended. Somehow, I'd momentarily forgotten my promise to myself to speak out, no matter the subject and no matter the stakes.

Most of the time, though, I remember to take a stand.

I've called people out for racism, Islamophobia, transphobia, and body shaming. A week after the aforementioned encounter, the same client made a similar comment and I replied "I value body diversity and respect people who can be unapologetically themselves."

No matter how uncomfortable I feel before speaking up, I'm always glad I did. Always. I'm no saint and I can't honestly tell you I'd be willing to risk my own personal safety for my principles, but I can say this: Exercising our values is like exercising our muscles. If we don't grow our capacity for advocacy and empathy when the stakes are low, we'll never have the strength to do so under high-stress, high-pressure situations.

If you're thinking Yeah, but it's not a big deal or people can say what they want or as long as no one's breaking the law, it's not for me to get involved, think again.

In the 1919 Supreme Court case, Schenck vs. United States, the Court determined that we are banned from false, dangerous speech that would incite a panic. For the life of me, I cannot understand why this prohibition does not extend to hate speech. Hate speech is false and it is intended to incite the endangerment of others. Even if our legal system hasn't exhibited the requisite intelligence to protect its citizens from shouting not that there's a fire in a theater, but that certain individuals are the fire, whose lives they intend us to extinguish, we as a social collective should advocate for greater verbal and emotional protections. Cruelty impacts people and feeling as if no one cares enough to come to their defense has a painful, often permanent impact.

In his 1963 "Letter from Birmingham Jail," Reverend Dr. Martin Luther King, Jr. wrote "We should never forget that everything Adolf Hitler did in Germany was 'legal' and everything the Hungarian freedom fighters did in Hungary was 'illegal.' It was 'illegal' to aid and comfort a Jew in Hitler's Germany. Even so, I am sure that, had I lived in Germany at the time, I would have aided and comforted my Jewish brothers."

King recognized that to stand for justice and equality means to take up the cause of anyone who is being marginalized. It" tempting to tell ourselves that it's not for us to get involved when the people who are being othered don't look, or act, or think as we do.

That's their struggle, we think. I'll save my battles for the people who matter to me.

This type of thinking is faulty, and I'm not just saying that because I believe in the interconnectedness of all humans or because I want equality for all. I'm also saying that out of my interest in *your* self-interest.

It's a misconception that hate can be compartmentalized. If you don't believe me, let's look more closely at the Holocaust.

Most people talk about the Holocaust in terms of the mass annihilation of six million Jewish men, women and children. They ignore the five million others who were murdered under Hitler's heteronormative Aryan agenda—gay, trans, lesbian, and gender queer people, priests, gypsies, communists, trade unionists, Jehovah's Witnesses, anarchists, Poles and other Slavic peoples, people of color, resistance fighters, academics, and individuals with physical or mental disabilities.

If we look at the Nazi's regime through the lens that it involved the persecution of one ethno/religious community, we miss the reality that eleven million unarmed and undefended individuals perished because of White supremacy. Hate is a virus. It spreads.

There is a famous poem by Martin Niemöller, a German theologian:

> First they came for the Jews
> and I did not speak out
> because I was not a Jew.
> Then they came for the Communists
> and I did not speak out
> because I was not a Communist.
> Then they came for the trade unionists
> and I did not speak out
> because I was not a trade unionist.
> Then they came for me
> and there was no one left
> to speak out for me.

Before I spoke with Holocaust survivors, their spouses, children, and grandchildren, I'd memorized the statistics—eleven million murdered, six million of them Jewish. But statistics couldn't capture the eviscerating impact of hate and it had never *really* sunk in for me, that had I been in German-occupied Europe between 1941 and 1945, I'd have been targeted because of nothing other than my race.

There is no way to remain professionally dispassionate when sitting with another human being, hearing about the worst moments of their lives, and knowing that, if you'd been born in a different time and a different place, you'd have suffered what they suffered or worse.

There were times during my interviews that I could barely speak. Others when I cried along with the person sitting in front of me. And I didn't just ask about the Holocaust. I wanted to learn about the person, how their life had been before and how it changed as a result of their pain. Trauma scrawls itself within our psyches in ways that others often attempt to minimize or dismiss, ways we ourselves struggle to articulate due to the perpetual pressure that wants every story to end with a happily-ever-after. It can be hard to witness the enduring ramifications of the past on the present, yet doing so can also be healing.

Marius Gherovici is a 91-year-old Holocaust survivor whose entire family was killed by the Nazis. His wife, Marta, joined him for our interview. As someone who knows and loves Marius, she provided invaluable insights.

"When we got married, Marius had terrible nightmares," she told me. "For me it was very shocking because suddenly he'd wake up in the middle of the night with his eyes absolutely open, but not be completely awake. And he'd be talking to me in German and Russian. He didn't know that he was talking to me. I don't know to whom he was talking. It was like that, night after night, for a long time, but then, with a lot of love, he was getting better and better and better. The ways we built our family, and built relationships with other people, that was what saved him."

Love may have saved Marius, but his path to healing hasn't been linear. It hasn't been complete, either. Marius is a whole person with a rich life and fulfilling relationships, yet trauma leaves a lifelong impact.

"You're always telling the happy ending story," he said. "You're always telling how you escaped and how you survived. The things you don't want to remember, you don't mention. I'm telling you everything that was successful. I'm not telling you what was not successful."

Marius' point is critical for his experience and also for the larger issue of divesting ourselves of responsibility for coming to one another's aid.

Personally, I hate when people say things like "Everything happens for a reason" or "Everything turns out well in the end."

No. By stripping our stories of the reality that people perpetrate horrific acts on one another because of their own irrational fears and hatred while other people fail to intercede, we're creating false narratives that keep us stuck in the status quo.

Part of what allows people—me, you, all of us—to remain disinterested in other people's pain is the perspective that everything will turn out alright in the end.

I want to encourage all of us to think differently. Instead of driving the narrative of *every person for themselves* forward, what would shift if we instead advanced the principle of tikkun olam (a governing tenet of Judaism that directs members of the faith to act constructively and beneficially)?

This does not mean that you have to spend every second of every day in service to others, but it means that, if you are privileged, it is your right and your responsibility to exert that privilege to make the world a better, safer place for others.

Alisa Kraut told me the story of her grandmother, Mina, whose town was invaded by Nazi soldiers. The Nazis arrived with their guns and began burning buildings, beating people, and enacting their cruelty with ruthless exactitude.

After they witnessed the destruction of their belongings and their homes, Mina and the other town inhabitants were made to march into the forest and dig a giant pit, guns fixed on them as they labored. Once they'd finished digging, the SS soldiers instructed them to strip naked and stand at the edge of the pit.

When the shooting started, Mina fainted and fell into the giant, gaping hole. She regained consciousness covered in dead, naked bodies. She awoke to the noise of glass shattering around her sounding to her ears like angels coming to her rescue. But, no. There are no angels on earth. There was only a Nazi soldier, staring contemptuously down at her.

Mina was so overwrought that she told the soldier to kill her, but he replied, "If you're not dead yet, I'm not going to shoot you."

He told Mina to run. She did and survived.

I'm not sure whether the Nazi soldier who spared Mina's life exhibited any other shreds of humanity to any other Jewish persons he encountered, but I know that, in that moment, he excavated enough empathy not to murder a naked, innocent woman.

I've heard it said that "there's bad in the best of us, and good in the worst of us." I believe that goodness comes from honoring the lives and the emotions of other human beings and that badness comes from desensitization and dehumanization.

When we allow ourselves to connect with someone else as a human being, we can't help but see them as significant. This humanization is something that we need to do early and often. According to research about how the brain works to recognize sameness and difference, our brains recognize difference and often have an initial reaction of aversion, while sameness offers a source of intuitive attraction. It is hypothesized that this has to do with the primitive and tribal nature of early humanity, where sticking with one's "own kind" and recognizing the danger posed by outsiders was essential to survival. Luckily, we can learn to override our initial impressions. The more we familiarize ourselves with different people, the more our prejudices recede. Love is innate. But the ability to demonstrate love, and to extend the scope of our emotional investment beyond our own immediate circle, has to be practiced.

In 2019, I visited the Knowledge Is Power Program (KIPP) school in Camden, NJ and Kellman Brown Academy (KBA) in Voorhees, NJ to interview students about their participation in "Names, Not Numbers," an oral history film project and curriculum created by Tova Fish-Rosenberg in which students learn about the Holocaust in a far more visceral and impactful way than they could ever hope to do through lecture-based or information-only instruction. With "Names, Not Numbers," students conduct in-person interviews with survivors, then create a professional-quality documentary using the direct testimony of survivors. The curriculum combines information, innovation, and empathy. To date, more than 6,000 students have participated.

My interest in "Names, Not Numbers" extended beyond Holocaust education. I also wanted to explore the connection between the KIPP School and Kellman Brown Academy.

The KIPP School's students are primarily Black and Brown and KBA is a Jewish Day school, so their students come from different backgrounds and have different life experiences. That said, if any of them had been living under the Nazi Aryan regime, they'd have been sent to concentration camps.

The middle schoolers spoke about the value of collaborating with contemporaries with whom they didn't initially seem to have much in common.

Max Scholl, an eighth-grader at Kellman Brown Academy told me that his KIPP School contemporaries "brought another perspective to the table, and so we had to research it with them and that helped us come up with more questions than we would have if it was just us."

Working together allowed the KIPP and KBA students to evolve beyond their own lenses. So did interviewing survivors. Izaneé Bryant of the KIPP School and Rebecca Lerman from KBA told me about sitting down with Goldie Finkelstein (whose son, Joseph, you'll have heard if you're a *Demystifying Diversity Podcast* listener). Both Izaneé and Rebecca said they wanted to cry when listening to Goldie recount the story of how the SS took her and her sister and, when her father went to get both daughters back, the soldiers told him he could only take one and made him choose between them. Goldie's father took her older sister with him and to leave his youngest daughter behind. He told her that, because she was younger and more childlike, he thought the Nazis would be kinder to her. Shortly after that, Goldie's entire family was taken to various concentration camps and murdered. While she was also taken to a camp, Goldie emerged alive.

I think it's essential for every one of us to ask ourselves the question: If I'd been alive and living in Europe during the Holocaust, who would I have been?

- A victim.

- A victimizer.

- A bystander.

- An upstander.

It's even more essential to ask ourselves: Who am I being now?

Today, being an agent of change can take a lot of forms. It might look like speaking out, offering a safe space, calling for help, chasing a perpetrator away, comforting a victim in the aftermath of an attack, and more avenues for intercession than I can enumerate.

Look at the example of Darnella Frazier, the seventeen-year-old minor who videotaped George Floyd's murder. If not for Frazier's critical evidence, it's likely Derek Chauvin, J. Alexander Kueng, Thomas Lane and Tou Thao would not have been arrested, Chauvin for second degree murder and the other three officers for aiding and abetting. It's also likely that public outrage over the senseless murders of Black and Brown Americans would not have reached the critical mass necessary to bring the Black Lives Matter movement into mainstream consciousness.

Prior to the death of George Floyd, there'd been forward movement for sure, but far too many had exempted themselves from taking responsibility for their role in maintaining systems of oppression. That shifted once people were confronted with undeniable evidence of racism in action and became personally invested in the lives and deaths of Black Americans.

Seeking to distance ourselves from the atrocities of the past only ensures that we will repeat those same, or similar, atrocities. Also, doing so is a blatant example of unchecked privilege in action. A Jew living in Nazi Germany couldn't exempt themselves from Aryan nationalism. Neither could a queer person, a gypsy, a Jehovah's Witness, or a person of color. Only someone who fit the White, cis-gendered, heteronormative mold of "acceptability" could opt out of the life-and-death struggle that was happening around them.

If they hadn't, if more people had stood up to protect the victims of bigotry and hatred, nowhere close to eleven million unarmed humans would have been killed by the Nazis between 1941 and 1945.

It's a privilege not to think about the Holocaust. Anyone whose family lived through it, or who lost family during it, continues to be impacted by generational trauma.

Alisa Kraut told me, "There are people who think of the Holocaust as the far-flung past to get over, but knowing that my father was born in a displaced person's camp and came over when he was a year and a half old, that makes it close to me."

The Holocaust should be close to all of us.

Long before Hitler spearheaded the annihilation of eleven million individuals, the rhetoric of Aryan superiority swept through post World War I Europe, specifically the countries that had lost the war, and been blamed for it. The anti-Semitic rhetoric didn't arise within a vacuum. Following World War I, Germany, Austria, and Hungary, were blamed for having started the war and the provisions of the Versailles Treaty forced them to shoulder the burden of paying damages to the victors. This created anger and despair that was then later exploited and used to spur on the scapegoating of Jews and other minorities. Also, the demoralization and public degradation of previously proud nations led to an upsurge of hate from those who felt they were being unfairly vilified.

We're seeing a lot of these same patterns of speech and thought with the White nationalist rhetoric that has proliferated in the United States since Trump began his run for office. A lot of Trump's propaganda-driven language and his emphasis on "making America great again" tapped into the feelings of disenfranchisement and devastation of the impoverished and demoralized White man and woman (I left non-binary individuals out of this because the vast majority of gender-queer Americans are vehemently anti-Trump, anti-Republican).

The more pervasive anti-Whiteness becomes, the more likely it is that there will be the kind of resultant responses we're seeing among White Americans desperate to protect their ideology and pride in their familial history. I find attempts to elevate Whiteness at the expense of Blackness despicable. I believe we need to create more conversations around empathy, tolerance, and the humanization of those on all sides of the various divides. I'm fairly certain that, if post-World War I Germans had not felt so attacked and so vilified, they would not have been so receptive to Hitler's anti-Semitic, anti-other propaganda. They wanted to feel as if they could be proud of their culture and heritage, and Hitler's rhetoric offered that.

We need methods of preventing victimization that don't encourage additional victimization and that foster empathy and cross-cultural understanding, also known as cultural competency. But the responsibility for developing such models shouldn't fall to the victim and are unlikely to come from the victimizer. The responsibility for effective intersession rests squarely on the shoulders of bystanders.

Gwen Borowski, CEO and cofounder of Philadelphia's National Liberty Museum, was the first to inspire me to think deeply about the role of the observer. When I went to interview her and visit the Forbidden Art Exhibition, a collection of 20 evocative images of art made illegally and under potentially grave consequences by Jewish and Polish prisoners in the Auschwitz Concentration Camp between 1940-1945, she told me that the purpose of the exhibition was to encourage visitors to think critically about their ability to use their agency in service of humanity. Borowski told me that it's critically important to stand up, speak up, and speak out against injustice.

"And," she said, shaking her head, "there's a lot of silence."

Even if your conception of yourself is that you get involved when it counts, you've born witness to an instance of victimization—from overhearing one person making an insensitive comment to another or to watching a bully beat someone up.

Let your mind go back to a time in which you chose not to get involved when you witnessed an instance of injustice. Now, ask yourself: If whatever you saw happening had been happening to the person you loved most in the world, and you'd been there, what would you have done?

When I interviewed Josh Perelman, Chief Curator & Director of Exhibitions and Interpretation at the National Museum of American Jewish History, he told me, "I'm not sure our job, whether as a museum or as human beings, is to heal the past. The past happened as it did. I think our job in the present day is to approach the past from a perspective of education and empathy, education meaning it is critical that we know our past, that we know what has transpired, especially in an environment that we live in today, which is 24/7 spin. But we also have to approach it with empathy because there are critical moral lessons to be learned."

If humanity could derive only one lesson from the Holocaust, my hope would be that we cultivate a greater capacity for empathy and that, from there, we put that empathy into action.

I sat down with Lewis Gantman, one of the Philadelphia board members of the Auschwitz-Birkenau Memorial Foundation, to talk about how the ABMF is striving to ensure that the concentration camp at Auschwitz is preserved in the exact condition that it was in on the day of liberation. I asked Gantman what motivated him to raise close to $1,000,000 for Holocaust remembrance. His response was to tell me about a section of every Jewish service known as the mourner's kaddish, wherein, on the anniversary of the death of a relative, congregants stand as a way of honoring their lost loved ones.

"I've started to stand for the mourner's kaddish every time I'm in synagogue," Lewis informed me, tears in his brown eyes, "because nobody's standing for the six million, and every day I'm there it's somebody's anniversary of death."

Louis Gantman has made the lives of those who died during the Holocaust so sacred and personal that he can't help but pay tribute to their memory.

Earlier, I mentioned my visits to the KIPP School and Kellman Brown Academy. Upon arrival at Kellman Brown Academy, I was met by Ellen Barmach, the middle-school Social Studies teacher who had contacted me to let me know about the project. A few minutes later, Ellen introduced me to Principal Rachel Zivic, a diminutive woman with a huge heart and kind, inviting eyes, who offered to take me on a tour prior to my sit-downs with the students.

KBA is beautiful and there's so much to notice about the school but, by far, I was the most spellbound by the long, central corridor. As we walked down the hall, origami butterflies of all different colors and patterns, fluttered overhead. There were well over a hundred, each one unique. Principal Zivic explained that, each year, every seventh-grade student selects the name of a child who died during the Holocaust, learns everything they can about that child's life, then creates a paper butterfly in their memory.

The project was inspired by the writings of Pavel Freidman, a young boy who wrote the poem "I Never Saw Another Butterfly" before being murdered at Theresienstadt Concentration Camp.

> The last, the very last,
> So richly, brightly, dazzlingly yellow.
> Perhaps if the sun's tears would sing
> against a white stone. . . .
> Such, such a yellow
> Is carried lightly 'way up high.
> It went away I'm sure because it wished to
> kiss the world good-bye.
> For seven weeks I've lived in here,
> Penned up inside this ghetto.
> But I have found what I love here.
> The dandelions call to me
> And the white chestnut branches in the court.
> Only I never saw another butterfly.
> That butterfly was the last one.
> Butterflies don't live in here,
> in the ghetto.

I don't believe that it is possible to care deeply about the lives of eleven million, or even six million people. It's too abstract a concept and our minds can't grasp the magnitude. We need to bring something too overwhelming to internalize (millions of people) down to a quantity we can feel—one.

Alisa Kraut told me something she tells her young daughter when acts of anti-Semitism, such as the October 2018 shooting at a Pittsburgh synagogue or the 2019 shooting in a synagogue in California, occur and her daughter asks "Why do people hate me because I'm Jewish?"

"I say to my daughter, they don't know you. They hate an idea. People that hate you for being Jewish, they don't know you personally. That's how they can do it. They've not made you a real person."

On the wall at Kellman Brown Academy, below the origami butter-flies, there is a written statement that every KBA student has memorized and that they all say out loud together each day: "I pledge to treat others with respect, use kind words, perform kind actions, stand up for myself and others, and be a seeker of peace."

I think those words should be a part of all of us.

Earlier, I referenced the principle of tikkun olam. I was first introduced to this concept by Deborah Baer Moses, founder of Theatre Ariel, a Philadelphia-based theatre company whose stated mission is to "illuminate the rich social, cultural, and spiritual heritage of the Jewish people."

"Through our history is a history of social activism of tikkun olam," Deborah informed me. "The obligation of repairing the world is a through line in Jewish religious life and spiritual life."

This obligation to repair the world ought to be adopted by Jews and non-Jews alike. And it requires many things, first among them getting honest about what is broken and what part we have played in enabling that breakage to occur, either through our direct action or our indirect lack of action.

Shortly after Bill Schwabe's 96th birthday, I met him, his aide, and his friend and fellow resident at his assisted living home, to accompany them on a tour of the Liberty Museum that Gwen Borowski and Lewis Gantman generously made possible.

The day was overcast and drizzly, but, when Bill arrived, he was all smiles. In the museum entryway is a replica of Philadelphia's famous Liberty Bell and people (mostly school children) love to pull its string and hear the resultant clanging. I asked if he wanted to ring the bell but he declined. The four of us and our kind and knowledgeable tour guide worked our way through the museum, moving from exhibition to exhibition, marveling at all the evidence of the human struggle for free-dom and liberty. When the tour concluded, before Bill and his entourage left, he told me, "I think I'd like to ring that bell now, Daralyse."

Bill motored his wheelchair over to the string attached to the heavy metal bell and pulled it so emphatically that the knell resounded throughout the whole museum. The tour guide laughed. "That's the loudest I've ever heard anyone ring that thing."

Bill smiled and rang the bell again. That was the first time Bill had left his assisted-living facility in years. It proved to be his last. He died peacefully in his sleep on July 7, 2020.

If you have the companion *Demystifying Diversity Workbook*, please turn to the exercises for Chapter 4 and start them. Return to Chapter 5 in this book when you have completed them.

5   **Unconditional Love**

"I identify as human, and I always have."
Dr. Nadine Rosechild Sullivan,
public speaker and diversity expert

It was their junior year in college when Oliver de Luz reached out to both their parents, separately (by then, their parents had divorced) to tell them that they were trans.

"I texted them both kind of the same message: I love you very much. I appreciate all the support you've given me. Just letting you know I'm trying to use this name now, so I know it will be hard and weird, but if you can just try, I'd really appreciate it," Oliver recounted. "My dad texted me back *Omigosh is Olly okay? I love you.* I love that. He was so positive. And I got a text back from my mom that said *No.* She sent another text: *What does that mean?* I had no answers, and she was demanding them."

Oliver was still in school, still under the fiscal care of their parents, and their mother used that financial vulnerability as leverage to attempt to strong-arm them into abandoning their non-binary gender identity. She had Oliver's phone shut off, refused to continue to contribute to their college tuition, and, according to Oliver's account, told them, in an email, "I thought my love for you was unconditional, but I realize that I was wrong."

Oliver and their mother no longer speak.

Now, Oliver works as a trans competency educator. They told me that they find it heartwarming when other children's parents approach them after their classes to say things like "My child is trans, how can I be a better ally?"

Oliver's answer is always, "The fact that you're even asking that question is a phenomenal start."

"If your kid is coming out to you, you need to be 1000% supportive," Oliver told me.

It's true. Whether it's your child, a family member, a friend, or even an acquaintance, if someone values you enough to be vulnerable with any element of their identity, it's a sacred moment and it's essential that you meet them with receptivity and love.

When I was in college at NYU, my only friend was Jimmy. We used to hang out in his room (on his bed), studying and complaining about, well... everything. He was a neat freak and his suitemates were slobs. His parents were overprotective and didn't trust him to make his own decisions. His roommate had broken one of his dishes (from the set he'd inherited from his dead grandmother) and refused to fess up about it.

I thought life was pointless, that there was no God, and that the universe was little more than a giant vortex swallowing our respective souls.

Neither of us understood Faust. We both considered Pynchon's work didactic. And, if asked about Freud, we'd have said that his reflections on women were pejorative and inflammatory and—more to the point—irrelevant in the modern context. You know, kid stuff.

We spent a lot of time doing homework, but we also went out. I remember roaming New York City streets in the middle of the night and smoking cinnamon-apple flavored Hookah at a local dive-bar, even though we were both underage. Jimmy and I were inseparable, except when the time came to eat or sleep. I was a practicing bulimic and did most of my eating in secret. In terms of sleep... I wished our relationship wasn't so platonic. True, I'd been dating the same guy on and off since high school, but I broke up with him every few months to go out with someone else. Despite my silent wish for Jimmy to come onto (and into) me, part of me was glad he hadn't.

I was too busy hating myself to love anyone else, and Jimmy was a good friend. I needed a friend.

Nevertheless, when he invited me to spend Thanksgiving with his family in Danbury, Connecticut, I declined. I didn't do Thanksgiving turkey and mashed potatoes. I'd wait until the day after, when no one was around, then gorge myself on leftovers, only to throw them up.

"Please," he implored. "I want you to meet my mother."

No guys had ever wanted me to meet their mothers—unless I was having sex with them (the guys, not the mothers)—and, even then, the word *want* was debatable.

"I'll come up the Saturday after Thanksgiving," I told him. (As mentioned, I had non-negotiable Friday binging/purging plans). "But I don't need an elaborate meal. I'd rather come for tea."

I arrived at the Smiths' cozy three-bedroom house on Campbell Lane in blue-collar Connecticut, and Jimmy's mother immediately wrapped me up in her expansive arms. It was clear she thought I was his girlfriend. She asked me at least a thousand questions about myself and told me at least as many fun facts about her son.

Did you know that...

Jimmy's favorite food is meatloaf?

Jimmy calls his grandma every Sunday? (He's such a good boy).

Jimmy is studying to be a lawyer?

Jimmy organizes his socks by color and length?

Growing up, I never had to ask Jimmy to do his homework? He always did it without being asked.

My friend was, in his mother's eyes, on par with the Messiah—only with better footwear and more fastidious grooming habits.

"I'm sure Jimmy didn't tell you that he's the first in our family to go to college. We couldn't be prouder."

"Wow," I replied. "That's impressive."

Together, we perused "adorable" baby photos of her beloved only child while that now-grown child mouthed "Thank you" and "I'm sorry" and "She's crazy" at me behind her back.

I didn't mind. I liked Jimmy's mom. Later, after he told me his secret, I didn't understand why he'd felt like he couldn't share it with her.

"You have no idea how good it is to meet you. My son can't shut up about you, and I can certainly see why."

Once Mrs. Smith and I had looked through at least a hundred photos and drunk three cups of tea apiece, Jimmy told his mom, and dad, and still-living grandmother, that the two of us were going for a walk.

"Should I pack you a snack?" She gestured at me. "This one's skin and bones."

He groaned. "Mom, we'll be back in an hour. People can go for an hour without eating."

In answer, she took a cookie from the center of the dining room table, popped it in her mouth, and chewed.

"Sorry about my family," Jimmy said once we were safely out of earshot.

"No need to apologize," I told him. "I like them. Especially your mom."

We strode to a clearing a little ways away from his childhood home then sat, facing one another, cross-legged, on the grass.

He was the first to break the silence. "Dara, I don't know how to say this... I've been keeping something from you."

I'd been keeping something from him, too. I was binging and purging and taking fistfuls of laxatives often enough that it was interfering with my finances and my health. I'd recently been admitted to Tisch Hospital after having seizures, the cause of which had been electrolyte depletion. As soon as the semester was over, I was going inpatient—again.

Jimmy didn't even know I was bulimic.

I reached over and took his trembling hand. "Whatever it is, you can tell me."

"I'm bisexual," he said. "You're the only person I've ever told."

Fear etched itself into his handsome face, but there was nothing for him to be afraid of. I admired his transparency and felt honored to have been the first person in whom he felt he could confide.

"Thanks for telling me. And for trusting me. I love you and I'm proud of you." I asked a few questions—like how long he'd known and what I could do to support him. Then, I said, "You know, Jimmy, if you're truly bisexual, I think that's great and I'm happy for you, but are you sure you're not gay and afraid to admit it?"

If I could do that moment over again, I would have responded differently. Although I happened to be right—my friend has been dating men (and only men) ever since—and he later told me that he said he was bi because he worried I might not accept him if I knew he was gay, that was his truth to discover and disclose.

In hindsight, even though I've always been attuned to the need for spectrum understandings of race, in that moment, it didn't translate into sexual orientation. It would prove to be a bitter irony considering that, in my twenties, I'd discover my own attractions were myriad and would come out first as bisexual, then later as sexually fluid.

When Jimmy entrusted me to be the first person he chose to come out to, I wasn't perfect. I was, however, open, receptive, and invested in our friendship.

When we get it wrong, which we will, it's essential to embrace each other.

Since that time with Jimmy, I've had others come out to me and what I've learned is that the best way to receive those people in their process has been to love them and to listen.

Oliver told me, "A lot of times in my competency trainings, people come up to me after and they're like, 'I have a transgender kid.' They have all of these questions, and they're like 'I wanna be the best mom I can be. I wanna be the best dad I can be.' And I'm like 'You're already so far ahead, just that intention and that willingness to learn is more than a lot of other people can say.' It feels really good to be kind of like a secondhand support to this child I've never met. I want everybody to have that, because I know what it's like to not."

I want everyone to have that, too. All human beings crave love, acceptance, and belonging. For members of the LGBTQIA+ community, that's not always there, and, sadly, when is it there, it's too often conditional or parsimonious.

I've had friends tell me things like "My parents told me they love me even though I'm gay."

This is terrible! Loving someone *despite* an element of their identity isn't loving *them*. If your child crashes your car and you love them anyway but require them to be more careful and pay for the cost of repairs, you're conveying the very constructive and reparative message *You're a good person who made a mistake and there's a clear path to restoring everything to all right again.*

This is perfectly reasonable. You have standards for your child's behavior. By enforcing those standards, you're reinforcing the values of responsibility, integrity, and honoring the property of others. Maybe your child feels temporarily guilty, an appropriate response when a person makes a mistake, but the guilt abates once they've taken the requisite action. And there's certainly never a lapse in love.

If you love someone despite one of their identity-markers—race, religion, sexual orientation, gender identity, physical or mental disability, or any of the other aspects of who they are and how they see themselves—what you're saying is "Something about you is inherently wrong and, although I'm telling you I love you, I wish you were different. And, because changing yourself would be impossible, my love for you will never return to its whole, intact, pre-coming-out version. You will either always be lesser in my eyes, or you'll need to go back into the closet and live a different life, or be a different person, than your authentic self." This is the message so many parents, spouses, siblings, grandparents, and friends convey to their supposed loved ones. It is a setup for shame and a brutal example of the way privilege operates.

The saddest thing about this, I think, is that these are the examples we look to of those who do a "good" job of reacting to their loved one's coming out. A fist to the face is better than a bullet to the brain, but that doesn't mean it's not also assault.

When I interviewed Dr. Nadine Rosechild Sullivan, an ordained interfaith minister and an instructor of sociology, gender, sexuality and women's studies, she told me a beautiful story of a happily-married couple that she interviewed for her dissertation.

This person was born with a penis and assigned male at birth despite never identifying that way herself. When she was old enough to attend kindergarten, the teacher would tell the girls and boys to line up separately. The girl, who had been misgendered at birth by her parents and society, kept being rebuked for lining up behind the other girls and forced to join the boys' line. By the time she entered high school, she'd had so many experiences of being forced to "get in line," both literally and metaphorically, that when she fell in love with the young woman she later married, they married as a heterosexual couple and build a seemingly cis-gendered, heteronormative life.

They had several children together and, by the time those children were in high school, their mother, who'd been forced by culture to identify as their father, found herself in her and her wife's bedroom with a revolver in her mouth.

"They were about 50-ish years old and they had told their wife back in high school when they fell in love and when they first started dating, 'Sometimes, I like to wear women's clothes,'" Nadine recounted. "And the wife had gone 'Okay. I'm in love with you, so I don't care.' They'd had almost twenty years of marriage and at this point, with the revolver in their mouth, they realized 'I have to transition, or I'm going to kill myself,' and so they came out of their bedroom and said to their wife, 'I have to do this,' and the wife said, 'Okay.'"

The woman who'd spent her whole life living as a man, and before that a boy, was subsequently able to get the requisite hormonal treatments and to transition with the love and support of her family.

"She was very blessed," Nadine reflected, "because many people in the time period in which I interviewed her, many trans women, were losing their partners. Very few people were staying."

Vara Cooper, a queer intersectional feminist, told me, "Dating trans people illuminates the pain and the oppression and the programming of patriarchy. I've watched trans people that I've had very strong feelings about really struggle and suffer with the male privilege that they were born with, or the male privilege that they were actively striving for. We have a long way to go for all genders. The programming, the patriarchy, it's hurting everybody. Even when we're cognizant of it and we're actively pursuing the gender and sexual identities that we want and that we idealize, that we glamorize, we're still going to have to pass through all these walls of patriarchy, external and internal."

Although the culture and the climate are shifting, in terms of greater awareness, greater visibility, more rights, etc., the world remains an excruciating place for many LGBTQIA+ individuals and some of the reason for this is that there's been a conflation of sexual orientation and gender identity with a presumption of immorality.

Identity issues can't be moral issues. A person is who they are and, if they tell you who they are, assume that they're right, that they've thought critically about it for a while, and that the question of their acceptability is not at issue. The real question is: Are *you* an acceptable friend, spouse, parent, child, colleague? Because, if your reaction is anything other than, "Thanks for telling me, I love you exactly the same," that's a problem and it's *your* problem—not the person who's taken the risk to divulge an element of themselves.

At NYU, I took a course called *Love the Sin: Sexual Regulation and the Limits of Religious Tolerance*, based on a book titled the same by Janet R. Jakobsen and Ann Pellegrini. Dr. Pellegrini taught the class herself and, not only was it incredible to learn material directly from the person who wrote it, I found the course, and the book it was designed around (or maybe the book was written as a support for the course—I never thought to ask) enlightening and useful as a way of understanding, then articulating, why we can't look at any consenting adult sexuality as a sin. I know that many people (possibly even you) have deeply held conceptions about what is and is not acceptable in terms of gender identity or sexual orientation. For some, these issues have become inextricably linked to their beliefs about eternal salvation, or damnation. It may feel completely anathema to even contemplate embracing an identity that your religion, or your culture, tells you is "reprehensible," but I would urge you to interrogate your misconceptions. That doesn't mean your religion is wrong, but that the interpretive lens through which you've been taught to see it (your learned bias) is.

I double-majored in English and Religious Studies and minored in history and something that not many people know about the most-often cited biblical passages "condemning" homosexuality are that they are, in actuality, condemning forcible rape, prostitution, and sex trafficking and do not relate to consensual, non-transactional sex. I don't want to get into a debate about anyone's religiosity, but a few books you might want to read about why, whatever your faith tradition, embracing LGBTQIA+ individuals is an enactment of your faith and not a detractor from it include:

- *God is not a Homophobe: An Unbiased Look at Homosexuality in the Bible* by Philo Thelos.

- *God and the Gay Christian: The Biblical Case in Support of Same-Sex Relationships* by Matthew Vines.

- *Transforming: The Bible and the Lives of Transgender Christians* by Austen Hartke.

- *Homosexuality in Islam: Critical Reflection on Gay, Lesbian, and Transgender Muslims* by Scott Siraj Al-Haqq Kugle.

- *Lesbian Rabbis: The First Generation*, Rebecca T. Alpert, Sue Levi Elwell and Shirley Idelson, eds.

- *A Rainbow Thread: An Anthology of Queer Jewish Texts from the First Century to 1969* by Noam Sienna.

- *My Buddha Is Pink: Buddhism from a LGBTQI perspective* by Richard Harrold.

- *The Man Who Was a Woman and Other Queer Tales from Hindu Lore* by Devdutt Pattanaik.

If your faith tradition isn't represented above, I apologize. And, if you are atheist or agnostic but still struggle with internalized prejudice, you might want to check out *Queer Disbelief: Why LGBTQ Equality Is an Atheist Issue* by Camille Beredjick.

In our families, our churches, and our interpersonal relationships, we have created imaginary ladders of worth wherein certain people are elevated above others because of whatever arbitrary ranking systems we've established. If the cultural climate has determined that anyone who engages in same-sex sexual relationships or anyone who is not cis is not "as" worthy, you have internalized the same set of beliefs that are responsible for the deaths of Riah Milton, Dominique "Rem'mie" Fells, Blaze Bernstein, Ta'Ron 'Rio' Carson, Ally Steinfeld, and countless others.

Love has to be inclusive, and it has to be unconditional, or it's not love. It's gas lighting. To tell someone you love them while also wishing their identity was altered places them in an impossible internal quandary. They're being assured they're being loved while, at the same time, feeling unaccepted. This is another form of perpetration and dehumanization that leads to the endangering of LGBTQIA+ lives.

Dr. Sullivan told me "Hate crimes against LGBTQIA people have only risen as we've gotten rights." This makes total sense. If a person has ranked certain individuals as lesser, it becomes threatening to see those individuals not just surviving but thriving.

Love is two-pronged. It is the set of sensations we feel and it is the discipline of taking actions that are commensurate with those emotions.

I understand that, whatever your individual belief systems, they were developed over time and will take time to un-develop, but even if it takes time and effort for internal beliefs to shift, behavioral changes can be immediate. That's fine. Loving people is even more rewarding when it requires us to stretch beyond our own personal agendas and abandon our outmoded attitudes.

If you tell someone you love them but are constantly slapping them across the face (and not as a consensual kink), your words, and even your feelings are irrelevant because you're not enacting love. It's the same thing with the gay, trans, queer, lesbian, and bisexual people in your life. If you say, "I love you, but don't bring your significant other to our holiday dinner," "I love you, but I can't endorse your wedding," "I love you, but I'm opposed to your gender-reassignment surgery," or "I refuse to call you by a different name," regardless of whether or not you feel love, you're assaulting an element of that person's identity.

Transphobia and homophobia are deeply embedded in American culture. They are reflected in our language and reinforced by our rhetoric, yet, if the hes and shes of the world don't make space for the zes and theys, we will continue to write certain people out of the script of existence. Not necessarily intentionally, but via the sin of omission. And the sin of othering.

After all, a cis person (someone who sees themselves as either squarely on the male or female side of the gender spectrum) can't comprehend why someone wouldn't want to be referred to as "he" or "she" unless and until they understand that there are gender identities that exist outside the cultural codification of male and female.

I want to be clear that lack of receptivity to queer identity and/or non-binary gender expression is not something that is restricted to those outside the LGBTQIA+ community. One of my interviewees, Vara Cooper, told me that she identifies as queer because "I'm not gay enough for gay people to accept me, I'm not straight enough for the straight people and there's a lot of biphobia, bi-erasure. It's like, 'Oh, pick a side,' or 'Oh, that means you're promiscuous.' Queer sort of pushes all of it. It says I'm amorphous."

Angela Gardner shared that "There are people in the transgender community who look down on crossdressers because human beings always love to have somebody they can point to and say I'm better than them."

"I'm better than them" is a way of saying "my life matters more than theirs," which is a precursor to the violence that is being perpetrated against LGBTQIA+ individuals all the time, and not only from people outside the community, but from those within it who've internalized the pain of being othered so much that they hate others and hate themselves. Like Kian Willis' killing of Patrick Sequeira-Ferreira. Or like the high suicide rate among members of the LGBTQIA+ community. In fact, LGBTQIA+ youth are five times as likely to commit suicide than their heterosexual contemporaries, and their attempts are five times more likely to be serious enough to require medical intervention, or to result in death. LGBTQIA+ adults are more at risk of suicidal thoughts and attempts as well, so much so that 48% of transgender adults report that they have considered suicide in the past 12 months, compared to 4% of the overall US population.

The internalization of rigid and narrow gender roles and the classification of certain forms of adult sexual expression as "good" and others as "bad" makes people believe that they have to be a certain way in order to be loved and keeps them from expressing their innermost thoughts and feelings, which leads to the belief that *If people really knew me, they wouldn't love me.*

Regardless of where we fall on any spectrum (sexuality, gender, race, religion, ability, body type...) we ought to be able to trust that those closest to us embrace us exactly as we are.

If you have an element of yourself that feels integral to who you are but are convinced that sharing it will make you less likely to be loved and accepted, or you have shared it only to be met with rejection, criticism, and a recitation of the catechism, you'll either start to resent those around you, or resent yourself. It's inevitable. For many people, it's untenable, which is why the suicide risk is so much higher among members of this community.

As Angela, who describes herself as two distinct individual entities ("I'm a dude and I'm a chick") put it, "You know, when you're seriously in the closet, you can't tell anybody and you don't know anybody else that does it, then you can get like really guilty and just messed up. Oftentimes, they talk about how trans people have all of these problems and it could all be fixed if they just fixed their gender problems, you know? Just get 'em cured. But no. The reason they have problems is that they have had all of this guilt, secrecy, and hiding. You know? I mean, when you're somebody that's really open and honest and want to be that way, but you've had this thing, and you've had to hold it and not ever talk about it, that gives you mental problems. So, in the case of trans women who want to transition and become women, they have found that giving them the gender surgery cleans up a lot of the problems that they've been experiencing."

As a social collective, and as the individuals who comprise it, we must practice the actions indicative of love. Not only is doing so the only way to true inclusivity, it's also healing and empowering. It forces us to confront our own biases, accept responsibility for the health of our relationships, and become better to ourselves and others.

Maybe you feel entitled to your judgments. You believe that you are right and that your way of being in the world is better than others. If they'd just be more like you, and less like themselves.

I'd ask you to sit with the possibility that many people, whose beliefs and judgments are diametrically opposed to your own, feel the exact same about their own prejudices and preconceptions. As much as you judge them for their rigidity and intolerance, what makes you so superior? Before looking outward, it's essential to look inward. Holding onto biases can have devastating ramifications for ourselves and for those we claim to love.

Oliver de Luz's mother forfeited her connection with her child because that child didn't conform to her rigid beliefs about gender. Wouldn't it be easier to let go of a belief than the person you gave birth to? What are you losing out of your need to be "right"?

I figured out a long time ago (the hard way), when I began to recover from anorexia and bulimia, that I couldn't hate myself into treating myself well. I didn't initially know how to enact love, but I've learned over time, through deliberate and diligent practice.

I had to take the actions commensurate with love and, eventually, the emotions followed. The same is true for our external relationships. We need to choose love, no matter our biases, and recognize that any inability to feel it requires an internal shift and nothing from the other person.

I thought it would be useful to offer a set of practices that can act as behavioral touchstones in the moments when you're at a loss for how to act towards others, or yourself, but know that you've made a commitment to choose love:

- Give your full attention. Be present with the person you're with.

- Anticipate their needs. Don't always wait to be asked to lend support.

- Let the other person know you're listening, by reflecting what you heard them say and modifying any objectionable behavior based on their feedback.

- Know their love language. Show love the way that they receive it and be receptive when they love you the way that works for them.

- Always make time. The one thing we can't generate more of is time, so giving yours is a way to show you care.

- Physical touch (if appropriate and consensual).

- Make eye contact.

- Be thoughtful and considerate.

- Tell the other person why they're amazing and what, specifically, you appreciate about them.

- Ask them what they want.

- Cheer them on.

- Accept what they have to offer.

- Have fun together. Laughter can offer a doorway into love.

- Practice radical forgiveness. Let go of what you're holding onto, or, better put, what's holding onto you.

In 10th Century China, there used to be a method of killing someone known as Lingchi, or "death by 1,000 cuts." Every time you shame or criticize another human being, or shame yourself, it's as if you are taking a blade to that person's flesh and delivering a small, but painful, slice.

I'd ask you to be the salve on your loved ones' wounds, rather than the source of them.

Rob O'Neil, improv comedian, writer, and movie connoisseur, had some useful reflections about what's needed from everybody: "We need to come to each other's defense when it matters. I think that's an important lesson for everybody to learn, especially now since everything's so divisive. We need to remember what we have in common because ultimately we're all playing for the same team, so, even if some of us are a little different, we have to make sure we have each other's backs."

When we begin our interactions from a place of loving receptivity, having one another's backs is easy. It takes practice, sure, and it's impossible to get it 100% right, 100% of the time, but one thing we can get right, from this moment on, is to make one simple but essential commitment: If someone cares enough about you to tell you who they are, value them and the relationship enough to say, "Thank you for sharing. I love you exactly as you are. Now, tell me how to best demonstrate that love. Tell me what, if anything, I can do to support you."

If you have the companion *Demystifying Diversity Workbook*, please turn to the exercises for Chapter 5 and start them. Return to Chapter 6 in this book when you have completed them.

6 Practice Being Anti-Racist

"Exposure and practice prepare young people, or adults, for unpredictable racial moments that can be highly stressful and can debilitate our sense of worth or our sense of inferiority. We practice scenarios that folks tell us they run into and we expect them to be mindful through it and also go over it often. Then we have them come up with strategies they wish they could have done, that they didn't do. There's a lot of research on behavioral rehearsal. The more you actually get a chance to go through and practice, the better you are the next time it shows up."

Dr. Howard Stevenson, Executive Director of the
Racial Empowerment Collaborative

Dr. Howard Stevenson was raised by two parents whose approach to dealing with racism could not have been more different. His father was from Southern Delaware, his mother from North Philadelphia. They were both Black.

"They had different strategies with how you dealt with race," Dr. Stevenson told me and my co-collaborator, AnnaMarie Jones. "My father's strategy was church twenty-four hours a day, seven days a week. Which means, you pray for people if they mess with you. More Martin Luther King-ish. Because my mother grew up in North Philly, she was embattled every day, so she was more Malcolm X. Her strategy was, if anyone bothers you, you can hit them or do whatever is necessary, violence is absolutely okay. So there was a lot of violence versus non-violence contention going on. When we talk about racial politics now, we think that people have to learn to be able to not only pray, think through, process, prepare—which is non-violent—you also have to be able to speak up and do something. You cannot simply be a processor and you cannot simply be someone who lashes out. You need skills in both."

As the Executive Director of the Racial Empowerment Collaborative, the Constance Clayton Professor of Urban Education, Professor of Africana Studies, in the Human Development & Quantitative Methods Division of the Graduate School of Education at the University of Pennsylvania, and Director of Forward Promise (a national program that works to improve the health of boys and young men of color and their families and to help them heal from the trauma of historical and present-day discrimination, dehumanization, and colonization), Dr. Howard Stevenson is a leading expert in the efficacy of various approaches to resolving racial conflict, both systemically and in the moment.

Today, we are seeing strategies of peace and strategies of violence being employed in various ways throughout our nation, and throughout our world. The aggregate effect is that action is begetting action. More people appear to be willing to acknowledge systemic racism and to call out the abuses that are occurring each and every day. Nevertheless, when it comes to issues of racial literacy, we are still woefully inadequate. In fact, for many people, racial literacy is a foreign term.

As defined by the Racial Empowerment Collaborative, "Racial literacy is the ability to read, recast, and resolve racially stressful encounters. This literacy can be increased via racial socialization strategies repeatedly practiced within a safe context (affection, protection, and correction) utilizing intellectual, emotional, and behavioral skills that protect and affirm racial self-efficacy (RSE), recast racial stress, and negotiate racial conflicts."

Dr. Stevenson's TED talk, "How to Resolve Racially Stressful Situations," does a phenomenal job of demonstrating the value of rehearsing for racial moments so that we can be better prepared to deal with them when they occur and to heal from their traumatic impact after they've already occurred.

One of my favorite lines in the talk is when he says, "our cultural differences represent the power to heal the centuries of racial discrimination, dehumanization, and illness." I believe that it is only by internalizing this as an essential premise that individuals (and the society we comprise) will be brave enough, and committed enough, to do the work of reconciliation. We have to first believe that difference is something to value, rather than something to fear.

Let's say you do already believe this. You might still wonder *why we should practice for racial moments? Shouldn't we eradicate racism?* Not only is it not that simple. To eradicate something that exists outside ourselves doesn't give us a sense of personal agency. Stevenson's work focuses on developing their racial literacy skills by rehearsing for situations, real and imagined, past and present, so they can act and react in ways that empower them.

"Being called a particular slur, having supervisors treat you differently than others as a function of your difference, those things hit you in places emotionally. I think it deserves the same amount of time to practice that as you would give to creating a lesson plan or doing algebra homework. You need the time to go over and over and prepare yourself for those moments emotionally," he said. He told us that he believes in rehearsing for racial moments over and over again until a person can answer the following question in the affirmative: "Can you make a healthy decision around a racial encounter in less than two minutes where you would feel as if you walked away holding onto your values, believing in your own sense of social justice, and having acted in commensurate with those values?"

I would argue that most people in this country, if asked whether they think less of people whose race is different than their own, or treat them as less valuable than members of their own race, would say no, and it's likely that they would be telling the truth—assuming certain sets of conditions.

Senator Sharif Street, of the Third Senatorial District of Philadelphia, told me, "There are a lot of people who will support policies that disadvantage most of the Black community who in their own personal lives are truly not racist people. Their kids may be in class with 30 kids and, in that class, there are 20 White kids, three Black kids, five Asians and two Latinos, and they treat all 30 of those kids equally, and would invite any of them to their house and treat them well, but those ten minority kids that are in that class all have upper middle class, highly-educated parents, too. That's why they're in that community. It's easy to say I'm going to respect and treat people equally who are already socioeconomically where I am but not recognizing that, because of historical racism, the majority of people of color are not in those circumstances and not in those communities."

With racism—interpersonal, intrapersonal, and systemic—our capacity for accurate evaluation and assessment is seriously skewed. One reason for this is that there seems to be an all-too-prevalent belief that racism is an issue of morality, rather than an issue of power dynamics.

According to Stevenson, "When we think about racism, we often think about it in terms of morality; bad people versus good people, good people don't do racist things. The problem with that is it neglects the history of how racism has been systemic in society. Prejudice, you can argue, is attitudinal and racism would be, what power do you have to enact that attitude of favorability or dis-favorability?"

We need to think about the power and the privilege that we have, not so that we can apologize or feel like bad people, or feel badly about the circumstances into which we were born, but so we can begin to use whatever advantages we have to stand up for ourselves and others using the strategies we've determined to be in alignment with our own values. We also need to be adaptable enough to amend our approaches based on the circumstances.

If I were to walk out of my front door tomorrow and witness a group of White supremacists attacking a person of color, I would either come out swinging a baseball bat, call the authorities, or enlist the support of my neighbors to help me intervene. If I were in a business meeting and another attendee made a racist remark, my strategy would be to verbally interrupt that individual and tell them why what they'd said was hurtful and how I'd like them to speak in my presence when moving forward.

In dealing with issues of race, we have to be intentional, and the only real way to do that is to actively engage in these sorts of situations through mental and emotional rehearsal.

There are several scientific studies that demonstrate, based on outcomes, the efficacy of mental rehearsal. Athletes who visualize themselves running a race or successfully sinking a free throw receive the same tangible benefits from thinking about their performance as they do from practicing. Likewise, practicing behavior in other areas, including interpersonal interactions, is key to achieving effective outcomes. This is why racial literacy and racial practice is key to achieving greater inclusion and to mitigating the negative impact of racism when and if it does arise. Anti-racism is a critical life skill that we have to study and practice if we have any hope of improving over time.

"If you can't figure out an algebra problem you don't necessarily say because I'm a good person, I don't think I want to do algebra anymore. Or, you can't have a parent come in and say, 'Look, my son really gets upset around fractions. He won't sleep, he won't eat, so for the next three weeks you're covering fractions, I'm going to leave him out of school and, when you get to integers, I'll bring him back, because I don't want him to be stressed," Stevenson said. "We don't approach other places of learning with, if it upsets you, you can opt out. So, the same is true around racial stuff. Just because it upsets you, BIG DEAL, that's not a reason to remain, incompetent or ignorant."

His example is illustrative. At the same time, mathematical competency and racial literacy are by no means equivalent skillsets. A person can navigate life without knowing how to do fractions. They might inadvertently miscount their change, or might not be able to balance their checkbook, or they might learn to make accommodations around their inadequacies, but it's unlikely that their lack of aptitude will have devastating ramifications for themselves or for others. Lack of racial literacy is far more problematic. Racism is as pervasive as pollution and even more harmful. We're all breathing in its ethers all the time. And this doesn't only affect minorities.

Paul Reese, graduate of Yale Divinity School, spoke to me about some of the deeply rooted philosophical investments in Whiteness that have serious and sometimes fatal consequences.

"There's a physician, Dr. Jonathan Metzl who wrote *Dying of Whiteness*. He is a doctor from Missouri and he went back to his home town and other small communities to address a lot of unnecessary deaths by suicide that communities are experiencing because of behaviors traced to racial prejudice. For example, the unwillingness to consider and study the impact of gun violence on these communities, and how the greater availability of guns there is associated with a marked plague of suicide by gun. Because guns are part of the fabric of the communal identity, while the amount of gun by suicide deaths is by no means acceptable to anyone who is struggling, as a family member or friend of someone who's died by suicide, these communities are unwilling to entertain the possibility that the gun could be the problem."

I'm not echoing Paul's reflections to debate the merits of gun ownership, merely to point out that our psychological investments in the "rightness" of our attitudes are leading to unnecessary deaths of members of every community, wherever the individuals that comprise that community may fall on the racial spectrum.

If you live in this country, you'll have heard about the wrongful deaths of Michael Brown, Eric Garner, Ahmaud Arbery, Breonna Taylor, and George Floyd. You may have even seen video footage of their deaths, or of the deaths of the many other Black and Brown Americans who have been murdered by police officers. There is an abundance of indisputable evidence proving the existence of racism and how the misappropriation of power along racial lines results in the senseless deaths of people of color.

I want to focus not on the situations that have done irreparable damage, the situations that resulted in loss of life. Instead, I want to examine a specific moment that incited public outrage because it is indicative of the way systemic racism has pervaded the psyches of so many people that even those who see themselves as liberal and anti-racist can and do sometimes weaponized their Whiteness.

The encounter between Amy Cooper and Christian Cooper (no relation) that occurred in Central Park on May 25, 2020 offers a powerful and instructive example of how internalized racism puts individuals at risk and, because, thankfully, it did not end in death (although it could have), I believe it can be more effectively utilized as a teaching tool.

Here's what occurred:

1. A Black man was bird-watching in Central Park.

2. A White woman was walking with her dog, off-leash, in direct violation of the park's posted rules.

3. The man politely reminded the woman of the rules and asked her to put her dog on a leash.

4. Instead of complying with the clearly posted regulations, the woman verbally harassed and attempted to intimidate the man.

5. The man responded by videotaping the woman's erratic and uncalled-for behavior.

6. The woman called the police, telling them in a histrionic tone that an "African American man" was threatening her life.

7. At no time did the man threaten the woman. In fact, he remained calm and conciliatory and even offered her dog a treat.

8. The woman continued to yell at and threaten the man.

9. Eventually, both parties left.

10. By the time the police arrived, they were gone.

The above course of events is a demonstration of unchecked privilege in action. Amy Cooper was doing what she wanted to do, against the rules. When Christian Cooper reminded her of those rules, she not only overreacted but her reaction put his life at risk. That's not an overexaggeration. Christian was in the park with binoculars. The wrong move and the police could have mistaken those binoculars for a gun, just as officers mistook Levar Jones and Philando Castile's wallets for weapons.

Because the police force is 77% White, racial biases that have permeated many of the psyches of those who have not been culturally conditioned to interact with Black and Brown individuals come out during the fight-or-flight pressure of law-enforcement encounters. Black men are 2.5 times more likely than White men to be shot by police, even though Blacks comprise 13% of the population and Whites 70%. It is a sobering statistic that one in 1,000 Black men will die by police officer.

I'm grateful that Christian Cooper was not in the park when the police arrived. I am also great that he videoed the interaction and that its going viral highlighted the problem of racism in America. At the same time, the social response wasn't corrective or restorative. Amy Cooper was fired from her job and vilified in the media, but that doesn't mean that she learned anything about how to be a better human in the future, or that others operating with the same misplaced sense of entitlement and racial superiority saw themselves reflected in her behavior and are doing the work required to change.

What if, after the video went viral, Amy were required to go to prisons and meet the many Black and Brown people who have been disproportionally incarcerated for the same low-level crimes as Whites who were never punished for identical actions? What if she were made to sit across from the mothers and fathers of Black Americans who were wrongfully shot by police while they were unarmed and forced to think about the possible ramifications of her hysterical phone call? What if she'd had to watch the video and chart out a step-by-step alternate course of action and take personal responsibility for each of her choices and mentally rehearse moments where she could have done things differently? What if her company, instead of firing her, had given her the option to continue working but to suspend her pay for six weeks and donate that income to a Black Lives Matter charity of her choosing, or, better yet, to any charity of Christian Cooper's choosing? What if, instead of dehumanizing her for dehumanizing Christian, we, as a social collective, made the decision to give her the opportunity to learn to be a better person and made that restorative process just as public as her non-instructive punishment turned out to be?

I see Amy Cooper's behaviors as the surface manifestation of a larger issue. The way we dealt with her actions did nothing to restore or rebuild. And, as we've seen, systemic racism has continued onward as the well-oiled machine that has been keeping our country moving forward since the cotton and tobacco fields built by the free labor of slaves, and now with the mass incarceration, preventable deaths, financial and educational oppression of Black and Brown Americans.

Unless we employ strategies aimed at education and empathy, we won't change the system and we won't change the individuals that comprise it.

All human beings—moral, immoral, or somewhere in between—have biases that they are not aware of. This is problematic even in the best of circumstances. It becomes even more so under high-stake, high-stress situations, life or death situations (such as officer-involved shootings).

After the incident between Amy Cooper and Christian Cooper, I heard a lot of language about how "bad all White people are" and "all those White feminists." Entire categories of people were presented as monoliths and as Whiteness was vilified we saw a simultaneous swell of White nationalist rhetoric,

I'd have liked to have seen more conversations about real, meaningful change and then the implementations of various solutions that would put that change into policy.

"The work of any reconciliation along the lines of the basis of identity require vulnerability, a vulnerability that we are told is not of value of the American way of being," Paul Reese explained. "There's part of me that wants to say just ignore the American way of being and just try it. The part of me that believes in the work that I'm doing says...that's so hard. It's so hard to share even a little of oneself with another being, because there is the possibility of being hurt. I won't claim to understand anyone else's pain because sometimes I can't even understand my own. The work of being present and vulnerable, learning how to tell your story, and the most important part...learning how to listen, really listen to someone else's story, and accept it for how it is presented to you and let it affect you and change you. I think that's the work we are trying to do."

There's a quote in Dr. Stevenson's TED talk, "There's an African proverb that goes 'the lion's story will never be known as long as the hunter is the one to tell it.'"

We're learning about systemic racism from the people who have benefitted from the structures of privilege that support it. This makes as much sense as getting advice about lung health from a tobacco company. *NO!*

Salaah Muhammad, podcast host, writer, and a self-proclaimed disruptor of the status quo, told me "You can't have these kinds of conversations [about race and systemic oppression] without understanding the original sin of our country which is slavery. We have never reconciled that as a country."

I'd like to return to Martin Luther King, Jr. and Malcolm X, strategies of peace and strategies of violence, of conciliation and of conflict. There is a time for both. But I believe there is a third strategy, a strategy that exists somewhere in the middle—a strategy of personal empowerment, through agency and action, combined with the simultaneous implementation of public accountability and civic engagement. We need to hold ourselves and each other accountable. This means talking about race, connecting with cultures outside of our own, reading and educating ourselves, practicing for various racial moments, lobbying our local, state and federal governments, voting with our consciences rather than our wallets, and making an unwavering commitment to continuing to do the work until we recognize that every color is equal and beautiful. Considering the conditioning that is systemically perpetrated on our social collective, we need to support people in seeing the beauty in others and in themselves. It's not enough to claim equity and equality. We need to empower people both to fight for themselves and to believe that they are worth fighting for.

The problem with Black nationalism as a response to White nationalism is that it still promotes the race-based elevation of certain people over others on the basis of race. I'm convinced that that's why, at the inception of the Black Lives Matter movement, that were a lot of well-meaning, but sorely misguided, people saying things like "all lives matter." There are actually still people saying this (although now it's less well-meaning and more deliberately ignorant). Whether its intentional or inadvertent oblivion, people don't understand that it can't be true that all lives matter until Black Lives Matter, because, as a social collective, Blacks are the most marginalized, disenfranchised and dehumanized members of American society. Additionally, there are other, non-Black marginalized communities that the Black Lives Matter movement supports. In standing in solidarity, BLM is demonstrating an investment in the lives of the most at-risk members of society. It is only when these lives matter that all lives will, in fact, matter.

On the other hand, there are a lot of problems that come with a "pray for each other and wait for hearts and minds to shift" approach. Offering prayers to a deity without taking action is a way of obfuscating responsibility. It allows people to say "I'm doing my part" when, in reality, they don't care enough about those they claim to care about to inconvenience themselves by actually taking a stand. And it can feel a lot like gaslighting to be told "I'm praying for you. I really want things to get better for you" by the same people who, through their unwillingness to take meaningful action, are enabling oppression to continue. Likewise, this prayer-only approach adds to disempower-ment and further perpetuates systemic disparities because it requires participation from perpetrators in order for change to happen. As long as bystanders refuse to intercede and victims lack the capacity to effect agency, perpetrators will continue to retain the power to exact systemic subjugation and the chains of oppression will remain unbroken.

"The only thing we can do to change people is to create structure that encourages the right type of behavior," Paul Reese told me. "Usually that happens in the format of legislation and finding ways for the government to reward positive behavior that results in the right type of behavior. If you really want to change the heart of racism, you have to change the heart of a person. That's the thing. You can't change anyone's heart, especially with an argument."

I refuse to wait for hearts to change. Instead, I encourage taking deliberate, consistent action towards interpersonal improvement, up-ward social mobility, racial literacy and justice for all. The approach I advocate is individual and collective. It requires cooperation by those who are willing to do the work. If enough of us are, I believe we will reach a critical social tipping point wherein diversity, equity, and inclusion become so normalized that anything else becomes an abnormality. For this to happen, we have to change public policy, something about which Senator Sharif Street is optimistic.

"Our public policy needs to always move towards both equity in the present and correcting the ills of the past," he told me. "If we can do that, I think, as a society, we're going to get better and better. American society really does, in the long run, as people become more sympathetic to other people's situations, become better. I'm encouraged that, in this space, over the course of time, that's going to happen."

If you have the companion *Demystifying Diversity Workbook*, please turn to the exercises for Chapter 6 and start them. Return to Chapter 7 in this book when you have completed them.

7 Agency

"I've found that people I've met on the spectrum come in all shapes and sizes. We're just a whole 'nother slice of humanity. I think the commonality, then, is not so much that we're all alike but, rather, we've had experiences of trying to fit in and not being able to do so because of the way the world treats us."

Steve Mallon, architect and autism advocate

On February 2009, Larry Rubin, the CEO of the Association for Adults with Developmental Disabilities (AADD), was standing in line at the Keswick Theatre, waiting to buy tickets to accompany his members on an outing to see a live musical performance by a Beatles cover band. Larry had gotten to the theater separately to surprise them and, when his members arrived, they were ecstatic.

"Larry's here! Larry's here!" they chorused.

The AADD came about because a handful of individuals with developmental disabilities and their families realized that, once children with disabilities entered adulthood, the system and society at large were failing them. They went from going to school and having regular interaction with their peers to a lack of socialization and a sense of stagnation. Socialization and a sense of community is essential for everyone and it's something that all too often is denied people whose ways of processing the external world are seen as falling outside of societal expectations. So the adults advocated for a chance to continue to grow and have fun and go places and have lives that went beyond sitting at home, watching TV, feeling excluded from life. The result of their self-advocacy was the AADD, an organization that provides recreational and learning opportunities that improve their members' qualities of lives through skill-building and social interaction.

The adults who disembarked from the bus in front of the Keswick Theatre ranged from 18 to their early 70s and experience a range of developmental disabilities from the very rare, such as Familial Dysautonomia, to the more common autism spectrum disorders.

There were hugs all around and then the AADD members went into the theater while Larry moved forward in line, eager to purchase his ticket and join the group. It was just before he stepped up to the counter that the woman in line behind him leaned over and stage-whispered to her husband, "Dear, I think we came the wrong night."

Larry was livid.

"It took every ounce of my wellbeing, but I told myself, 'teaching moment,'" he recounted, ten years after the fact, when we had our interview. "I turned around. I said, 'Ma'am, you are not going to have to worry about my people. They will sit quietly. If it's time to sing and clap, they'll sing and clap. If it's okay to dance in the aisles, they'll do that. They're a very polite group. You're going to have to worry more about the people in your own section. I left. At intermission, the woman found me, shook my hand, gave me a check for $100 and said, 'I'm really sorry.' I taught somebody that everyone belongs."

Larry's recollection of the events that occurred at the Keswick Theatre touched me deeply, but also unsettled me. It's the rare individual who has the presence of mind not to react in anger and, instead, to keep their critiques constructive and informative. There need to be more Larry Rubins in the world. But I can't help but feel that the woman didn't learn the real lesson. For her to have internalized that would have required her to engage with the people she'd prejudged based on her misconceptions about what it means to be a person with a disability. The apology and donation might be evidence of limited learning on behalf of the theatre-goer who openly othered the members of the AADD, but my hope for anyone reading this is that what didn't happen can provide insight into how individuals with developmental differences are so often divested of their agency.

"It's not about us without us," Steve Mallon, a now-retired former architect, father of two, told me. Steve was diagnosed with autism in his 50s and has a lot to say about how many people do what the woman in line did, both when she was being actively pejorative and while she was apologizing and handing Larry a check.

Steve and I spoke at length about the very particular problem of lack of interpersonal agency in disability advocacy. "Neurodiverse people need to be empowered to be their own advocates, rather than having people advocating for them, prescribing for them, legislating for them, structuring programs for them. Let the neurodiverse people be their own advocates and give them the means to be able to do that."

So often, individuals with disabilities are not given the opportunity to engage in the conversations that directly impact their lives. They are kept out of discussions and interactions that involve them. I'd noticed this even before I began to explore the topic more in depth, but I had no idea how pervasive it was or that it's not just people who are outside the community but often allies and supposed advocates who fail to engage directly with those they claim to be helping. That's not the case with Larry at all. He has deep relationships with his members, whom he views as extensions of his family. He told me about a brief stint he spent in the hospital during which one of his members called him, every day, to check in.

"He called me more than my own kids. This work, being with these individuals, has so enriched my life... Sometimes, I can't help but cry. I'm so grateful."

Speaking with Larry was both heartwarming and heartbreaking. From the moment he answered the phone, I knew that those with developmental differences are being ignored and overlooked and that more of us than we care to admit are complicit. I've been working as a journalist for a while now. I've interviewed more than 100 people. Any time I've called any other individual or organization, the sequence of events has been as follows: I'll reach out to make initial contact, explain my project, and either leave a message, be given a time and date for an interview, or be told, "thanks, but no thanks."

When I called the Association for Adults with Developmental Disabilities, the receptionist put me on hold for fifteen seconds, then the CEO of the organization came on the line and informed me that he'd cleared his schedule and was willing to talk for however long I wanted. "Or," he said, "If this isn't a convenient time for you, let me know what is. I'll make myself available whenever you need."

"Excuse me?"

I couldn't believe my ears. The AADD currently has 160 members ranging in age from 18 to 74. Larry Rubin is the organization's Chief Executive Officer. Yet, here he was offering unlimited access to his insights and his schedule. He even gave me his personal cell number.

"When I heard there was a journalist on the phone, I was so excited," he said. "I can't tell you how many media outlets I've reached out to, but no one ever calls back. You have no idea how impossible it is to get journalists to talk about these issues."

By the time I reached out to the AADD, I'd done enough due diligence to know about the historical mistreatment of individuals with disabilities to know that we are a long way from equity and agency, but I'd thought we were, as a whole, getting better. We're not.

One of my closest friend's daughter is autistic and she has had to take her child out of the Greenwich, Connecticut public school system because she was being physically harmed by her classmates. To complicate things, because her daughter has a limited capacity to communicate verbally, the abuse went on for months before anyone realized what she was trying to communicate about why she hated school and didn't want to go. Instead of taking responsibility, and corrective action, even after the school was made aware of what was happening, the administration downplayed the abuse to avoid the possibility of a lawsuit.

Is this really where we are as a social collective? Our schools care more about money than the safety of the students we entrust into their care.

School can be a painful place for those with developmental differences, whether now or 50 years ago. Of his elementary days, Steve Mallon told me "As a child, I was knocked unconscious. I was urinated on. All kinds of things happened. It was really tough and my mother wanted me to be a little diplomat. She wanted me to go back out there and take control of the situation, make friends with people. I didn't want to go outside. I didn't want to be involved in that world."

By "that world," he meant a world of homogeneous expectations, a world that made it unsafe for him to be himself.

Steve had to continue to enter into an environment that was both physically and psychologically damaging and he still caries scars.

In the case of my friend and her daughter, the abuses stopped. Safety was reestablished. But not by the school system. It was financially viable for my friend to give up her professional career and become a full-time caregiver. This isn't an option for many. And, even if it were, parents shouldn't have to relinquish their careers to ensure their child isn't being beaten up every day for being different. And what constitutes difference anyway?

It is estimated that one in five Americans have a disability, making individuals with disabilities the largest minority group in the U.S., yet they are still being left out, or openly othered.

As part of her own self-advocacy journey, Marta Rusek has come out as on the spectrum both personally and professionally. "When the election of 2016 happened and we now had a president who not only mocked a person with a disability, but we also had someone in the DOE who was hellbent on rolling back funding the right of children with disabilities that are trying to learn and get an education which is their right to do," she told me. "That's really when I began to be loud and proud about being an autistic woman."

Now, four years later, Marta has written and spoken extensively about the importance for inclusion. In her September 2017 article "Autism Found Me and Then I Found My Voice," she wrote:

> While I am open and proud of who I am, I am also very much aware of the obstacles that prevent other adults from receiving a diagnosis and treatment for autism. Statistics and support are more widely available for children than adults. (A 2012 figure from the CDC says that one in 68 children have been diagnosed with autism spectrum disorder, but I could not find a concrete

statistic for adults living with autism in the United States.) And medical professionals are misdiagnosing women and girls because the current testing model is based on findings from studies conducted almost entirely on boys.

There are other factors that set my path to diagnosis apart, namely that I am a [W]hite woman who grew up in a middle-class household and received a good education in spite of my learning struggles. I have been raised with the idea that nothing is out of reach for me, and I had good health insurance and worked for a supportive employer when I received my diag-nosis. The same can't be said for many individuals on the autism spectrum who are African-American, Latino, immigrant, or transgender, who experience discrimination at a disproportionately higher rate than [W]hite cisgender women like me.

People on the autism spectrum are also at greater risk of experiencing domestic violence and sexual assault, and the incidence of suicide in the autism community is alarmingly high. This makes sense when you understand the social isolation and communication difficulties that afflict adults living with autism...

Each of us has our own learning style, and we all com-municate and process information differently. And each of us is struggling in a way no one else can possibly understand. But facing that struggle in a world where we know we are valued, loved, and accepted makes it much easier to face it and talk about it.

Marta acknowledges that hers has been a privileged existence, and, at the same time, that being a person with a disability in a world that is intensely and intentionally ableist, has been a challenge. There are more barriers standing in the way of her ability to exert her personal agency and demand rights then there ought to be, but she also has more support than many individuals on the spectrum. For her, advocacy requires a lot of mental and emotional labor, but she feels safe within her skin. Not everyone experiences that.

"I learned to shut down and keep my mouth shut," Steve recounted, "because, if I engaged at my level, they would threaten me."

Steve still finds it difficult to use his voice. He is a gifted singer, but there are moments when he'll be on stage during a performance and freeze. At those times, he takes comfort because he is in a choir. He says being surrounded by other singers, even in the rare instances when he finds himself without a voice, provides him with a sense of belonging. He never felt he belonged anywhere until he reached adulthood. It's taken a long time and a lot of support to get to this place—not that Steve can't navigate the world, making his own accommodations and developing tools and tactics that support him, but because there have been innumerable times when the world says "No. Your way isn't okay with us. You don't fit."

When he worked in corporate America, he had a difficult time with the overhead fluorescent lights (which have been demonstrated to trigger migraines, skin irritations and eye sensitivity in many), yet when he began wearing sunglasses at his desk, so he could focus on his computer screen, his coworkers ridiculed him and HR reprimanded him. Ditto when he built himself a makeshift screen shield. On his own time and at his own expense, Steve constructed an apparatus that diffused the glare from his computer screen and the higher-ups at his company insisted that he take it down.

For addressing the needs of those members of our community whose ways of thinking and acting don't fit within the arbitrary boundaries of conventionality, our inadequacies are glaring. Sure, rights and legal protections have changed and there are social protections in place to keep from the sorts of abuses—institutionalism, social ostracization, medical experimentation—that we once perpetrated against people who did not conform to mainstream expectations. But there is still considerable devaluation of individuals with disabilities.

Imagine having a worker who is innovative enough to construct a glare-diffusing apparatus (and does so at no cost to the company), then formally reprimanding that person, instead of recognizing the potential asset of having someone whose neurological wiring allows for those sorts of out-of-the-box solutions. Steve dealt with a lot of depression and a high job-turnover rate because, despite being a diligent and dutiful employee with an innovative and dynamic brain, he was perceived as weird and ostracized by the very corporation that his innovative thinking could have benefitted. This was a loss to his employers and also to Steve.

"It's really good to make sure that your occupational lifestyle is good," David Clizbe, PhD, a biomechanical researcher, engineer, teacher, entrepreneur, and the identical triplet of two brothers with cerebral palsy, told me. "Because what we now understand is that people have a better quality of life when they have something that they can go do and earn a living. We want people to be able to be the best them that they can be."

It's an important part of a person's identity to feel not only that they have something to contribute but that their contributions are recognized and respected. And it provides a sense of stability and a solid support structure.

Larry Rubin sees the tangible benefit of equal opportunity for his members and their families all the time. He told me that it's as if the parents and caregivers of his members breathe a sigh of relief when their loved one finds a job they enjoy. "Independence is what all parents want for their children. They want them to be independent so, God-forbid, when they pass, they have either places to stay or people to take care of them. They want them to have a social life and friends, and they want them to be accepted into the community. I think jobs are the main thing. If we could have more employment opportunities, the world would be great."

If, instead of saying, either implicitly or explicitly, "Because your ways of filtering and interpreting information are not conventional, they are not valuable," we invited people to share out-of-the-box solutions, the world would be much better. Unfortunately, there is a lot of infantilizing of individuals with disabilities. And this infantilization and devaluation often happens by people and organizations you'd least expect it from: people and organizations who claim to be advocates for the community.

For example, in the height of irony, multiple sources have reported that the group Autism Speaks has been openly condemned by over 60 disability advocacy organizations for failing to adequately represent autistic people and for their exploitative practices. Maybe the organization ought to rethink their name, considering that the techniques employed by Autism Speaks perpetuate autism silence.

When organizations with wide-reaching influence fail to include the individuals they claim to serve in meaningful and constructive ways, they are, in essence, disabling them.

As David Clizbe put it, "This has to do with all humans. If you remove agency, someone's essentially disabled."

Steve Mallon told me, "I think one thing neurodiversity has to offer is to give the rest of the world a bigger picture of humanity." And this bigger picture is valuable.

Matthew Newell, co-founder and director of the Family Hope Center, expert on brain health, and the father of an adopted daughter with early-childhood neurological and developmental challenges, agreed. Not only does Matthew see people of all ages achieve a sense of agency and autonomy (which society tells them and their loved ones isn't possible) daily as a professional, he has personal experience with refusing to allow societal perceptions to dictate what is achievable.

In the early 1990s, when Matthew's daughter was in third grade, all the teachers told him and his wife to keep their expectations low.

"She'll never surpass a third-grade reading level and she'll never be able to overcome her challenges."

When I asked Matthew how he reacted, he said, "I knew it wasn't true. I've learned that people are quick to determine neurological ceilings, for others and ourselves, and when we do that, we miss out on all that people have to offer."

Matthew's daughter ended up being a high-level collegiate athlete, graduated with honors, and is now a lieutenant in the fire department while simultaneously continuing her education to obtain her physician's assistant degree.

Without fail, every person I spoke with about developmental disabilities emphasized the disservice we do by underestimating and excluding neurodiverse individuals, a disservice that not only hinders the individual themselves but also hinders society as a whole.

"Everybody's on a spectrum," Steve told me. "There's no such thing as normal. People think differently and, if you try to force people to think in the same way, there are going to be outliers, and then you're really cutting off a huge amount of human potential."

Our ability to demonstrate our human potential exists in direct proportion to our ability to effect agency over ourselves and our lives. Stacey Cunitz, a director of college counseling with a private practice as an independent educational consultant, told me that the primary aim of support interventions ought to be to assist people in "growing their own self-advocacy skills so that they can handle life with little to no scaffolding."

For some, scaffolding will always be required. As a person who has had my own mental and physical challenges, I make modifications around my needs on a daily basis. Just because someone has certain limitations, or sees the world in unique ways, doesn't mean they're not equipped to live lives of personal fulfillment and social contribution.

Some people see those with developmental differences as less capable and less valuable and exclude them on that basis. As stated previously, this belief exists in individuals who are actively discriminating against individuals with disabilities and in those who advocate for them supposedly on their behalf but without involving them. We can't perpetuate the infantilization of grown adults.

The Abstract of the important 2011 paper "Infantilizing Autism" by Jennifer L. Stevenson, Bev Harp, and Morton Ann Gernsbacher reads as follows:

> When members of the public envision the disability of autism, they most likely envision a child, rather than an adult. In this empirically based essay, three authors, one of whom is an autistic self-advocate, analyzed the role played by parents, charitable organizations, the popular media, and the news industry in infantilizing autism. Parents portrayed the face of autism to be that of a child 95% of the time on the homepages of regional and local support organizations. Nine of the top 12 autism charitable organizations restricted descriptions of autism to child-referential discourse. Characters depicted as autistic were children in 90% of fictional books and 68% of narrative

films and television programs. The news industry featured
autistic children four times as often as they featured autistic
adults in contemporary news articles. The cyclical interaction
between parent-driven autism societies, autism fundraising
charities, popular media, and contemporary news silences adult
self-advocates by denying their very existence. Society's overwhelming proclivity for depicting autism as a disability of
childhood poses a formidable barrier to the dignity and wellbeing of autistic people of all ages."

Something I found heartbreaking was discussing how societal
stigmas around the capabilities of those with developmental differences
can strip them of opportunities to pursue dreams that might include
romance, love, and family.

"I don't think there's adequate focus on an adult with disabilities
parenting or enough support and resources and a lot of that is because
of bias," Melissa Tsui, outreach manager for Action for Early Learning,
told me. "For the longest time, if people had a disability, they were
discouraged from having kids. Hopefully, we've moved past that, but
still... Right now, it's kind of like you're lucky or you're not. You're
lucky if you have a family that can provide support or are at a certain
income level, but in general we don't have very good societal supports."

It is at least partly due to the all-too-prevalent practice of seeing
disabled Americans as children, and therefore incapable of doing and
wanting all the things other adults want and do, that individuals with
disabilities aren't provided with adequate resources to support them in
childrearing and employment. Many people with disabilities are being
divested of individual agency and often report feeling as if those that
ought to be allies aren't supporting them in advocating for themselves.
To be an ally is to be invested in the agency and empowerment of
another person or group of persons, to demand rights, rather than
restrictions.

I want to return to Larry Rubin, standing in line when the woman
said, "Dear, I think we came the wrong night."

Larry was right in informing the woman of her erroneous
expectations and, in fact, the woman took a step in the right direction
by apologizing and attempting to contribute. However, this small
action wasn't nearly enough and isn't an effective model for others to
emulate.

If she wanted to learn a lesson, the woman should have struck up a
conversation with one of the members of the AADD, or joined them in
the aisle for a dance.

There is tremendous beauty in interacting with a whole host of
people who have varying perspectives and varying ways of navigating
in the world, but there's no way to access this beauty without operating

from a space of equality and inclusion. The way forward has to involve agency, and we can only create space for agency for others if we abandon our illusions of superiority—and if we begin to have authentic interactions with people we deem to be different than ourselves.

Change comes through exposure, interpersonal interaction, and the deliberate dismantling of outmoded beliefs. Ideally, these beliefs would never have the opportunity to develop in the first place, which is why inclusion beginning at an early age and continuing throughout our lifetimes is essential. The earlier we can teach people to interact as equals, the less unlearning they will have to do as adults.

When I was in school, people with developmental differences were sent to other classrooms—maybe even other schools. There was very little exposure and, had I not had friends with family members with disabilities, I never would have had conversations or played games or interacted with people whose minds and/or bodies operated differently than mine. I was so fortunate.

Upon first impression, it might appear that including individuals with disabilities in mainstream classrooms, and everything else society offers from youth through adulthood, would be solely beneficial to the person with the developmental difference. But that isn't the case. Melissa and I talked a lot about how and why children with developmental disabilities being amidst typical learners is valuable for all.

"If you're a typical learner in a classroom, it's fine to be around a lot of other typical kids and you're going to learn a lot, but you're not going to learn what you'll learn being in a class that includes children with disabilities."

Melissa explained that being amidst nontypical learners encourages neurotypical children to think in more expansive, flexible, dynamic, and adaptive ways.

"Those are amazing skills," she pointed out. "Those are social skills, but they're also professional skills in a lot of industries."

I think all humans should aspire to be lifelong learners, which is one of many reasons why including all people in meaningful, valuable, equal and engaging ways should not end in childhood. We want to invite full and active and complex participation and recognize others' capabilities and the value that is inherent in variance. We can't isolate people, separating them into silos, and we can't have inclusion without recognizing and supporting agency and self-advocacy.

"When someone is trying to speak about you, without you, things can go horribly wrong," Marta informed me. "That's why you'll hear phrases like 'not about us, without us!' Making decisions about a particular community, in this case the autism community [or other neurodiverse communities], that decision should really be made with the direct input and feedback of somebody who is going to be impacted by it."

We need to center the voices of individuals with disabilities, not only in terms of disability rights, but in terms of the larger conversation about how to improve our nation and our world. We need to be asking "What do you want? What do you need? How can society be better?" while recognizing that no group is a monolith.

Seeking to empower individuals and to encourage advocacy for any minority that places that minority at the center of the work is essential. We need to stop believing that we know what others need, and we need to stop fearing differences. Until we do that, we miss out on the incredible gifts that individuals offer, not despite their differences but because of all the various factors that comprise them, exactly as they are.

"I think in any situation, if it's a decision being made, we need to be in the room as part of that discussion, so that nobody is having their civil liberties trampled upon, making sure that the information is accurate, and that the solutions, if there are any solutions that are warranted, are going to be as inclusive as possible for people who are on the spectrum," Marta told me.

David agreed. "The thing that makes people able to keep going is having a way that they can shine their light."

People want to shine their light and want to trust others to appreciate it, not snuff their light out.

I remember, when I was younger, my mom asked me to clean my room or something, and I told her that, if she loved me, she'd do it for me. Her reply, which she delivered with a smile, is still as clear to me as it was thirty years ago: "Daralyse Rebecca Lyons, I do love you, which is why I want you to learn to be independent."

Matthew Newell said it well, "Anytime you incorporate love into an equation, you get results, but love needs an action plan. The action plan needs to be delivered in a way that the patient, the child, the human being is trusted and feels a part of the process."

If we hope to make the future better than the past, we need to begin—immediately—to allow individuals to determine their own needs. Then, it's incumbent upon us to support and equip them for success—to provide temporary or permanent scaffolding without inflicting shame or feeling a sense of superiority. I believe that we have to love each other enough to fight against the impulse towards uniformity and conformity. After all, the social collective is only as valuable as it is varied.

If you have the companion *Demystifying Diversity Workbook*, please turn to the exercises for Chapter 7 and start them. Return to Chapter 8 in this book when you have completed them.

8 Belonging, Inclusivity, and Culture

"Everybody makes mistakes, but you want people to recognize that your character is based on the religion that you practice. If you have a beautiful character, you have a beautiful religion."

Aliya Khabir, Principal Consultant,
AZK Communications, LLC
(Public Relations and Diversity Training)

Asma Rehman was born in the United States. She grew up in the Midwest. She listens to Beyoncé and Lady Gaga and is a huge fan of the TV show *Downton Abbey*.

Asma loves shopping, sends her friends (including me) gifts for holidays, birthdays, special occasions, and "just because." She starts our phone conversations with "Guuuuuuuuuuuuuuurrrrrrrrlllll... I have so much to tell you."

We've spent hours talking about life, love, work, and current events. When I don't know what's happening in our country because I've been holed up in my apartment writing, she fills me in on the latest happenings and texts and Instagrams me pertinent articles. She has an abiding love for the values espoused by American democracy. Each year, on the Fourth of July, while I eat take-out at home and watch *Curb Your Enthusiasm* reruns, she barbeques and watches fireworks exploding in the sky.

Though Americanness is interwoven into the fabric of her identity, she realized after the 2016 Presidential election that there are many who, because of a different piece of fabric, consider her to be an other.

"When the language in our country was shifting during the election, I, for the first time, started to feel really othered," Asma told me. "I had never thought of myself as not American, ever in my life, until then. Yes, I'm different than the regular Joe Shmoe, but that doesn't make me not American. I went through kind of an identity crisis, because, if I didn't belong in the country that I was raised in and loved, then where do I belong?"

The Rehmans are, in so many ways, the example of the "ideal American family." Asma has a brother and her mother and father are still married after more than forty years. The family of four, equally Pakistani and American, has a rich, full life in Kansas City. But, because my friend wears what is alternately referred to as a headscarf, a khimar, or a *hijab*, there are people who consider her to be a threat.

"Growing up, I always felt American, because I am American," Asma continued. "There's so many identities to me, but I was always American. For me, the beauty of this country is that it brings people together from all over the world and all different walks of life."

Like so many other Muslim women, in the wake of Trump's election to office, Asma found herself suddenly fearful. Earlier that year, during an interview, then-Presidential candidate Donald Trump had said, "I think Islam hates us." And one of his first acts in office was to sign an Executive Order banning foreign nationals from seven predominantly Muslim countries from visiting the country for 90 days, indefinitely suspending entry to the country of all Syrian refugees and prohibiting any other refugees from coming into the United States for 120 days.

Asma is the National Chapter Manager at the Council on American-Islamic Relations (CAIR), the nation's largest Muslim civil rights and advocacy organization. On a professional level, she deals with the ramifications of Islamophobia on a daily basis. But she said it wasn't until the election of America's 45th President that she felt personally at-risk for an element of her identity. It's no wonder. FBI statistics show that hate crimes against Muslims grew by 67% in 2015, the year in which Trump launched his campaign. According to a Pew Research Center analysis, the number of assaults against Muslims in the United States between 2015 and 2016 surpassed the peak reached in 2001, the year of the September 11th terrorist attacks. From the presidential primaries and in the aftermath of Trump's election, and still today, Muslim women were verbally and physically assaulted. Some assailants attacked their victims while evoking the President's name.

The Muslim women I interviewed told me of the time when Trump began his ascension that they couldn't remember such rampant Islamophobia since immediately after 9/11 when 19 members of one extremist group perpetrated an attack that in no way is representative of the beliefs of the approximately seven million Muslims living and working in the United States today. Yet the media and the government responded by vilifying Islam. It's unconscionable.

According to psychiatrist Dr. Mona Masood, 9/11 marks a moment in American history when the wearing of a headscarf became imbued with a different significance than it had ever had before.

"Prior to 9/11, it was very personal. My religion was very personal, and I really wanted the hijab to be a representation of me. It was very much about that. After 9/11, women who wore the hijab had to make a conscious decision about not only being representatives of themselves, but of the religion. In the community, I remember, there were conversations about whether or not women wanted to wear it anymore because now it represented something more than they wanted it to. When a person is wearing a hijab—for us it's not the end goal—it doesn't symbolize that we have reached some state of spiritual excellence. It just represents one piece of a person's journey. So, all of a sudden, people were questioning... Well, what does this piece [of cloth] mean to me anymore? Maybe, somebody was doing it for modesty. Maybe, somebody was doing it for identity, like me. Now, it had to be a representation. So we had to go out there and now anything we did would not only be a representation of ourselves but of the faith."

As a practicing psychiatrist, Dr. Masood's role is to support her patients in exploring their emotions and enacting their agency. She and I spoke about how challenging it can be to express one's individuality (considering that all individuals operate out of a multitude of intersecting identities) when they are perceived as nothing other than a single identity marker. This is a challenge she has seen in her patients and also faces herself.

"I remember a supervisor of mine, when I was in residency, he was a psychiatrist, just very bluntly said, 'So, what do your patients think of your hijab?' I said, 'I never asked.' He actually challenged me on that. He said, 'I want you to remember, it's not *if* your patients are thinking about your hijab. It's *what* your patients are thinking about your hijab. It's there. As much as you want people to see all the intersections that make you who you are, that's what they are seeing first. You have to understand that, because you have to understand, when they are talking to you, they are filtering things based on that. Whatever information they are bringing to you, in the back of their mind, that is important to how they are conveying their message.' I thought about it and I thought, *He has to be right.* I started to become aware with small things. I'd be talking to a patient and they would apologize for something like cursing, and I'd be wondering *Why they are apologizing for cursing?* Then, I'd realize, *Oh. They must assume that I'm a person who doesn't curse. Where are they getting that impression? Probably from the hijab.* Then, instead of waiting for these moments to happen, I would ask them, 'What does it mean to you that your psychiatrist is a woman who wears a hijab? What role does this'" (she gestured to her headscarf) "'have in the room?'"

"I really convinced myself that, by speaking without an accent, by dressing in a certain way—maybe not the hijab, but everything else—by being able to follow the cultural trends, by being able to use the idioms of now, all of that made me American" Dr. Masood told me. "I think, in a way, I was trying to convince myself that I am just as American as everyone else. Then, when that was brought up to me, it forced me to really understand that there is actually this barrier, whether I want to admit it or not."

By the time I began this particular series of interviews, I knew all too well the devastating impact of othering and the systems of oppression that perpetrate it, but Islamophobia is distinctly different. I'm not looking to rank oppressions. All oppression has devastating and potentially deadly ramifications. Nevertheless, it's essential to point out that the prejudice perpetrated against Muslims in America has been so socially-sanctioned, media-publicized, and politically and legally enforced that, at the same time as they're being victimized, they're simultaneously being portrayed as victimizers. Why? Because this particular subset of Americans has not only been portrayed as different, but as dangerous.

Every time a Muslim person commits a crime, the news media emphasizes their religion when describing the perpetrator, as if religion had anything to do with the reason for their infraction. The reverse is almost never true. We don't turn on the TV or radio and hear "a Christian man...", "a Jewish woman...", or "A Buddhist human..."

As a journalist, being confronted by the egregious representation of Muslims in the media has challenged what I believed about the level of integrity and competence of my professional peers. Not all of them and not for all issues; but it was a sobering realization nonetheless that the media has done to Muslims what the police have done to Blacks. The persecution has been relentless. According to a June 2016 article in *International Communication Gazette*, "Media representation of Muslims and Islam from 2000 to 2015: A meta-analysis," found that while Islamophobia significantly increased in the USA between 2004 and 2008, this trend was not observed in Europe. They add that anti-Muslim prejudice in the USA is increasingly associated with anti-Muslim media discourses. These prejudices against Muslims were specifically driven by security threat perceptions in the media."

Because two of my interviewees, Hediya Sizar and Aliya Khabir, have specific expertise in media relations, speaking with them was incredibly illuminating. They provided concrete examples of media-propagated Islamophobia.

In her NYU honors thesis, "The Depiction of Muslim Americans in Children's Literature: A Case Study on the Children's Imprint Salaam Reads," Hediya demonstrates a myriad of ways that the inculcation of Islamophobia operates within White mainstream American society and how it pervades everything from media targeted towards adults to the books and movies enjoyed by the most impressionable among us—children:

Stories created by the dominant group perpetuate many negative stereotypes of Muslims and lack cultural authenticity, which ultimately makes integration difficult into the larger U.S. society... These negative stereotypes and misrepresentations dominated American television and films in the 1970s and 1980s and continue to be ingrained in contemporary picture books based upon these characters. The film *Aladdin* (1992), for example, depicts Jasmine and Aladdin with 'light skin, American speech patterns, and Anglicized features' and characters such as Jafar with dark skin, greed, and evilness (Furman, 2014)... When young children have an inaccurate understanding of Islam and the Middle East, they can develop a subtle form of racism towards the religion (Fox and Short, 2003). For children who identify as Muslim, there is a possibility of developing a false consciousness towards themselves and Islam. Not only does children's literature feature orientalist stereotypes of Islam that influence the way dominant groups of children perceive Muslims, but eventually, these stereotypes influence how Muslim American children perceive their own religion.

Non-Muslim kids grow up being bombarded with images and characters, or caricatures, that reinforce anti-Islamic rhetoric and then grow up to be adults who carry those same views with them. Often, they have no interactions with Muslim individuals and those controlling the narrative aren't familiar with the people they're depicting.

Nihad Awad, the Executive Director and co-founder of the Council on American-Islamic Relations (CAIR), the largest non-profit Muslim civil rights and advocacy organization in the United States, had firsthand experience with negative depictions and unfair representations of various communities and told me that seeing those depictions of others, specifically through Hollywood portrayals and in the news, was a driving force behind his decision to abandon engineering and become a social justice advocate. "Let me tell you the impact of negative portrayals of communities by Hollywood. I was born and raised in a refugee camp and we did not have electricity or TV except, maybe 15 years later, my family got a black and white TV. I was obsessed with watching American movies, and most of the movies that I saw then depicted African Americans as savages, violent and sub human. Likewise, Indigenous Americans. They were portrayed as the enemies of the United States, as vicious people, even as animals, devoid of spirit or value. Even at the time, I knew that was wrong, but I did not have anything to counter it. In the movies, there were all these White people, looking nice and talking nicely and when I eventually came to the United States and began to meet and interact with different people from different communities and joined the Muslim Students Association on campus, I started to have firsthand experience and discover the beauty of other people and to see all of us as brothers and sisters. Perhaps, the biggest surprise was to see then how my people had been depicted in American movies and on the news as vicious, sub-human and violent. I saw this terrible and unfair representation of my community and my people. I resolved to push back against racism. It's important to take a stand."

Aliya Khabir is actively taking a stand to change portrayals of Muslims in the media. She became involved in media relations at a time when there were no in-house Muslim reporters, fact-checkers or staff writers at any of the Philadelphia or Delaware Valley news outlets that contracted her as an occasional consultant, which meant that a lot of the information that was disseminated was not only false but inflammatory.

"A couple of years ago," she told me, "there was a man who went to the mosque for the evening prayer. He prayed the evening prayer, he walked out of the mosque, literally walked up like three or four blocks, pulled out a gun and shot a police officer in his car just out of nowhere. This action was the result of a mentally ill person who shot a police officer, and the shooter just happened to be Muslim. There was no reason for the FBI to come and investigate, yet, all of a sudden, it became a national story. So it was my job to go to the mosque and prep that Imam and prep the people who go to that mosque and monitor the press conference and make sure that the Muslim community was getting a fair shake. I was not going to allow them to turn this into a terrorist action, because it wasn't. The documentation showed the man had been mentally ill for years and had been on and off medication. People find religion and try to find solace and ways of treating all sorts of illnesses. The fact that the shooter was Muslim should not have played into this because, if he'd left a church or a temple, instead of a mosque, his religion wouldn't have been an issue. This wouldn't have been in the media as a national story. It would've stayed a state or local story. This man left a church and shot a cop. But, when someone leaves a mosque, all of a sudden, he's a terrorist and it's a national outcry. No! I was not going to allow that to be the story line."

Because of the conflation of Islam in the media with certain acts by a few individuals who took actions that were not in keeping with the principles of the Quran, there has been a widespread cultural conflation with Islam and terrorism. Not only is this ludicrous, it detracts from the real problem—the simultaneous villainization and victimization of Muslims.

Muslims aren't terrorizing America. America is terrorizing Muslims.

As Nihad Awad told me, "Islamophobia is not something of the past. Islamophobia is active. Islamophobia has been mobilized and normalized by powerful people in our society. It is becoming normalized and empowered by people like Donald Trump. Throughout his election campaign and into his administration, he's been taking direct shots at the Islamic faith. And, obviously, when you see the President, your President, promoting xenophobia and Islamophobia, he's given a green light for people to commit discrimination and take actions against the American Muslim community."

Physician Suzanne Barakat delivered a powerful and evocative TED talk, "Islamophobia killed my brother. Let's end the hate," in which she recounts how her newly married brother Deah, a basketball fan with a desire to help the world through his dentistry and philanthropy, was shot execution-style along with his wife Yusor and sister-in-law Razan. The murder was a hate-crime. The three unsuspecting victims were preparing to eat dinner at Deah and Yusor's Chapel Hill, NC home when a neighbor, Craig Stephen Hicks, knocked on the door.

Craig Stephen Hicks forced his way inside and executed Deah, Yusor, and Razan based on nothing other than his own Islamophobia. He had previously threatened Yusor and had been posting anti-Muslim rhetoric and spewing hate-speech all over his Facebook page, but, when he turned himself in to the police, Hicks claimed that he'd killed Deah, Yusor, and Razan over a parking dispute. There was no dispute— parking or otherwise. Nevertheless, the police released a premature statement to the media who then ran with a false version of the story provided by the victimizer which intensified the victimization of the three young murdered Muslims.

As Barakat orated powerfully from the stage, "They were murdered by their neighbor because of their faith, because of a piece of cloth they chose to don on their heads, because they were visibly Muslim."

To be visibly Muslim in America means, in many contexts, to be seen, but never really known. According to a 2016 Brookings Institute poll, nearly six in ten Americans don't know a Muslim personally, yet 41% of Americans have an unfavorable view of Islam. How can you view someone unfavorably if you've never taken the time to inquire about them?

This isn't to say that no non-Muslim Americans have cultivated curiosity and connection. Many have. That's probably why Islam is the fastest growing religion in the United States. The faith offers quite a lot in this life and the hereafter. One element that is of especial attraction for converts is a chance to shed the shackles of their past.

"Look at Malcolm X," Aliya told me. "He didn't want to have the name of the family that owned his family as slaves. So, a lot of Muslims, when they convert to Islam, they kind of want to shed everything that they had before and that includes, sometimes, a name. When you say, 'Ash-hadu an la ilaha ill Allah. Wa ash-hadu ana Muhammad ar-rasullallah,' what happens is, all of the sins that you have accumulated all the way up to that point, are wiped clean. You are a brand-new person. You are like a new baby, with brand new experiences. And people usually want to choose a name, just like Mohammad Ali chose a name when he left Cassius Clay behind." The name was an expression of his freedom and his faith. (It is interesting to note that Aliya was named after the famous American boxer).

One of the most iconic athletes of all time was Muslim and he was a civil-rights advocate, a humanitarian, a catalyst for social justice, and a philanthropist. He was also an American cultural icon, referred to as the "GOAT" (Greatest of All Time), and he achieved all this after converting to Islam, yet many have developed the twisted conception that Islam is somehow un-American.

Asma is one of my closest friends and, since we spend a lot of time together (or did prior to the COVID-19 pandemic and will again when restrictions lift), I've been with her at events where entitled White men have displayed such flagrant insensitivity by moving to hug her even after she's told them that hugging strangers of the opposite sex is something she chooses not to do as part of her commitment to her faith. I have literally thrown my body between her and these would-be huggers because they wouldn't honor her simple request to avoid non-consensual touch. Many of the women were weird, too, not under-standing that the prohibition didn't apply to them and avoiding physical contact in such a way as to make me, and I'm sure her, although I didn't ask, uncomfortable.

Even some of the "attempts" at connection have struck me as slaps in the face. I've never heard about a Jewish or a Christian person being asked "What do you people do in your culture?" as if they were viewed as a part of a homogeneous collective, devoid of difference on the basis of their religious beliefs. But I've been with Asma three distinct times when it did. Once, I blurted out, "Stop acting like she's supposed to be a representative of her faith, as opposed to a person." Another time I pulled the asker aside, whispered my thoughts on their lack of thoughtfulness, and they apologized. And on the last occasion, Asma had a direct and deliberate confrontation with the person in which she explained that he'd been inadvertently insensitive and that, maybe, he could rethink his delivery.

"When somebody says to me, 'This is what we do, what do you do in your culture? And my answer is 'But my culture's American. What do you mean, my culture?' You know, that is othering because they're centering their experience as the norm and what I do on the Fourth of July is we go see fireworks, and we barbecue. We do the same things that you do, and it may look a little bit different, but my culture is American culture," Asma told me.

She's gotten so used to subtle micro-aggressions and exclusionary attitudes that it rarely fazes her, although it can be exhausting to contend with. As Ahmet Selim Tekelioglu, Outreach and Education Director for CAIR-Philadelphia, informed me "Many American Muslims will negotiate aspects of religiosity. Let's say you're in a meeting and you want to pray, do you say, 'I need to go out and pray for five minutes,' or do you just say, 'I need a five-minute break'? And, for women who wear the hijab, they have to negotiate what it might mean for their professional life or sometimes for their safety."

Between 2012 and the time of this writing, there have been close to 800 documented incidents of anti-Muslim persecution and discrimination in America. And these are only the reported cases.

"We see that people become desensitized to even the discrimination that they face," Ahmet said. "There is actually underreporting of racial abuses that many people of color experience. There is severe underreporting and it's sad. In a focus group from one of our chapters in California, students said, 'Look, I'm called names in school. They make explosion sounds when I walk into a room. They call me Osama. When a helicopter passes over, they say 'The police are coming for you,' but I'm not going to report it, not because I'm afraid that I'll be called a snitch, but because my relatives are being butchered in Syria. They are running for their lives. Why would I cry over someone calling me a name? I'll just deal with it.' Or, here [in Philadelphia], in an urban setting, where there is so much gun violence and economic insecurity, sometimes these things are put to the backburner because they know there are many more vital issues they or their families are facing."

Ahmet and I spoke about how micro-aggressions can feel like death by 1,000 cuts. As excruciating as they are, it is often daunting to deal with every individual injury. At the same time, these micro-aggressions can often lead to these macro aggressions because they speak to an underlying level of othering, hatred, or dehumanization.

"It's important to make sure these things don't go unchecked," Ahmet said.

We can't keep allowing ignorance to fuel intolerance.

Federal Bureau of Investigation statistics show that only 5% of domestic terrorist attacks involve a Muslim culprit, yet law enforcement agencies and media outlets regularly represent members of the faith as dangerous. Following the 1995 Oklahoma City bombing, because of police and media misrepresentation, a Muslim man was originally arrested.

"When the Oklahoma City bombing happened," Asma told me, "I don't know if you know this, but a Muslim man was arrested initially." I didn't know. Because I'm not Muslim, I have not had to be cognizant of and hypervigilant to the same things as my friend. I haven't had to worry about whether, following every act of domestic terrorism, I might be at risk. Asma continued. "It was really bad. The Muslim community really suffered because of that. We were in Islamic school at that time, and my mom was teaching there, and we had somebody shoot, with a gun, the front door and windows of the Islamic school where there were children, all the way down to preschool, because they thought it was a Muslim who had done the Oklahoma City bombing."

Timothy McVeigh, the Oklahoma City bomber, is a White Christian man. And White Christian men are responsible for the vast majority of domestic terrorist attacks. Yet, that is not something that's generally spoken about.

If people took the time to expose themselves to the teachings of Islam, and how individuals integrate those teachings into their lives, I'm convinced that it would incite widespread and lasting positive change. But, so far, that hasn't happened. According to the Islamic Networks Group (ING), 62% of Americans report that they have never conversed with a Muslim.

I encourage you, if you're among that 62%, to learn more about the many extraordinary individuals who attribute their philanthropy, advocacy, and commitment to justice to the very faith that has been erroneously depicted by so many as un-American.

One of the most consistently egregious depictions of Islam has to do with how women are portrayed. When he was still a Presidential candidate, Trump criticized the mother of a slain Gold Star soldier, openly berating the woman for choosing not to speak and standing silently while her husband delivered a powerful message. Trump insinuated that the grieving and heartbroken mother's decision not to speak publicly was evidence of Islamic oppression when, in fact, it is the rare parent who can find their words in the wake of the death of a child. But Trump played on a pre-existing Islamophobic trope about Muslim women not having power or agency. There are cultures all across the world where patriarchy has and continues to oppress women, Muslim or not, but in those nations where women have rights and freedoms and agency, Muslim women are incredibly empowered.

"I just think that there's such a huge misconception that women who wear hijab are oppressed. Honestly, it's so silly," Asma reflected. "If people were to actually know Muslim Hijabi women, and know how powerful Muslim Hijabi women are, they would never think that."

Using the term *hijab* to refer to a khimar or a headscarf began after 9/11 due to an error by the media when they began referring to headscarves as hijab. In fact, the word hijab refers to a modest style of dress, a style applicable to all genders.

Few people outside the faith community know what the head covering worn by many, but not all, Muslim women signifies, or that it signifies different things to different people. People wear these symbols of faith and submission to God for a multitude of reasons that no one but themselves may ever be privy to.

For Dr. Mona Masood, "Wearing hijab, specifically in this culture, in the American culture, for me was a conscious decision that I made when I was fourteen years old. I was the only one in my whole family who wore it. My father's the only man in our family. It's three sisters and my mom. For me, at the time, at fourteen, my parents were not exactly supportive. They really questioned why I was doing it. Because their experience and one of their reasons for pursuing medicine was a way of having relevance in this society, of being respected in this society. They wondered, did I not want that too? That was probably one of the first instances that we started unraveling the issue of what it means to be a first-generation immigrant in America. They were feeling like maybe they didn't understand their own child. I told them wearing the hijab—and the reasons have evolved—but, at that time, it had been about (and this was prior to 9/11 that I chose to wear it) that I wanted to identify as Muslim. Because we were living in North Carolina and we had moved there from New Jersey, I was getting a lot of stereotypical bullying about not understanding what my skin color meant and where I was from—a hodgepodge of stereotypes. I really needed it to be known that I'm not only brown, I'm this particular faith. It became a need for identity. Over time, it has taken on a more spiritual element of modesty and humility and checking ego and remembering we are part of a vast network and society. I feel like still today, and this is my opinion of Hijabi culture, it serves as an identifier. There is a need in the Muslim community, especially among my generation, of needing to be proud of who we are. I think most Hijabi women in the United States would say it's important for them to be recognized as Muslim."

For Asma, wearing a headscarf is a symbol of being Muslim, a demonstration of her dedication to God, and something else as well. "When I wear hijab, when I wear a scarf, and when I'm in hijab, which is like in modesty in general, I get to choose what I share with the world and what I don't. For me, having that agency is hijab."

Aliya Khabir emphasized the feeling of connection through community. "Doesn't matter where I am," she said. "I can look out into the world and find another Muslim." Aliya also loves the vibrancy and the variety of Muslim fashion options and the opportunities for expression of self and of culture. "I've been in all kinds of situations, receptions, and conferences, and what have you, and people are truly amazed at a very fashionable Muslim woman because, what they've been exposed to on the news, from like the 1970s all the way up until now, is the negative images of Muslim women, who walk ten feet behind their husbands, dress in black and are not allowed to show their faces. What you have to understand is, that's all patriarchy. Islam doesn't require that. Last year, I performed the Hajj with my brother and my father. I was in Saudi Arabia basically the whole month of August. It was so beautiful to see all the Muslims and their different colors because they're from literally every country on planet Earth. We were all performing the highest rituals, the prayer rituals, and we were all different ethnically. We were all from different backgrounds, we were all dressed differently, but the concept of our dress was the same. Everyone was dressed modestly."

I wish more people could have a window into the beauty of Islam in action and be gifted with the opportunity to observe and appreciate the values espoused by the prophet Muhammad.

"Islam is not here to box you in and tell you, you can't, because that's kind of how it's been sold in media. That women can't do this and children can't do that, and can't, can't, can't, can't," Aliya told me. "Islam is not a bunch of rules. It's a lifestyle that maximizes your experience as a human being. You will get the max experience out of being Muslim while you're on this earth in preparation for the hereafter."

The values of free will, agency and liberty are core to the foundation of our nation and it is staggering that so many people who know nothing about Islam have either intimated or outright said that the religion is un-American. Another key concept of the faith that offers tremendous value to the social collective is its emphasis on civic cooperation.

"Community is front and center of our actions," Asma explained. "Giving back is a huge, huge, huge part of our religion. There are many different cultures that are a part of Islam. There's so many countries all over the world where Islam is practiced. So, within people's own personal cultures, which go beyond religion, it may look different but a foundation of the faith is that you must take care of your community. That is paramount in our religion, and it's very clear."

Aliya concurred. "In Islam, justice is a foundation. Justice not just for Muslims, but justice for everyone in humanity. As a Muslim, I have to call myself out if I've done something wrong to someone, Muslim or non-Muslim, and I have to right that wrong. It is a part of our foundation to eliminate oppression, eliminate injustice, wherever it is and however it is being implemented."

She explained that "Islam gives us three ways that we can contribute to a call [for justice, equity, and inclusion]. The first is that you can take action. The second is that you speak out against injustice. And the third is that you hate it in your heart and you pray for it to be alleviated. The third is the weakest of it, but, if that's where you are, to continuously pray for the oppressed to be relieved of that oppression, that's what you do until you find the strength to speak out against it, until you find the strength to change it with your hands, whether that means going out and registering to vote or protesting in the street."

There are no perfect religions because religions are comprised of people and not a single one of us is faultless. As comedian Dave

Chappelle, who is Muslim, once said, "I don't normally talk about my religion publicly because I don't want people to associate me and my flaws with this beautiful thing. And I believe it is beautiful if you learn it the right way."

It would be ridiculous and disingenuous for me, a devout agnostic, to advise anyone to convert to or from any religion. At the same time, I stand humbled and inspired by the individuals I have met who practice Islam. Even though so many of my people (journalists) have been so unkind to so many Muslims, no one within the Muslim community has ever prejudged me or treated me as anything other than an equal and a friend. Those I know well and those I don't have welcomed me with open arms—me with my unruly, uncovered hair, decidedly immodest outfits, and lifelong love of bacon. I've enjoyed learning about Ramadan, the daily calls to prayer, the emphasis on family and community engagement that are part and parcel of the faith. Why, I asked, weren't more people aware of all the beauty that Islam has to offer? Why do so many of our elected officials and media outlets present such a skewed picture of a system of beliefs and personal disciplines that can and do offer so much to this broken democratic system?

One of the challenges afflicting Muslims in America is that their voices are not being centered. The voices that are being centered are voices of individuals who are ignorant about Islam. My hope is that the sense of American culture can expand to include all the beautiful and varied individuals who comprise it. But that can only happen if we open our minds and hearts, and if we do what Islam advocates—pray for justice, speak out against injustice and do our part to bring about change.

If you have the companion *Demystifying Diversity Workbook*, please turn to the exercises for Chapter 8 and start them. Return to Chapter 9 in this book when you have completed them.

9

Appreciate, Don't Appropriate

"It seems to me that, when you're talking about studying diversity, you can approach it vertically and/or horizontally. Vertically, you talk about a particular people, a particular culture, a particular community, and you go backwards and then forwards, to see the internal evolutions and changes, to see how different things have been born—how different things have come into being out of the same root. Horizontally is to go outside a particular cultural community, a particular society, cast a wide blanket, and try to understand how different peoples, societies, and cultures have looked at essentially the same things."

On-cho Ng, head of the
Asian Studies Department at Penn State

Paul Reese was shaken. They could feel the reverberation of their heart, beating the drum of panic. The incident was over, yet its impact remained. How could that officer have been so reckless? How could they have had no recourse? The encounter spoke to a larger pattern. Paul had experienced it before. Each time, it hurt.

Like so many Asian individuals, moving about the world being treated like they are somehow perpetually un-American, an outsider, can be soul-eviscerating. Or it can inspire a person to take action.

Paul Reese sat down at their desk, took a deep breath, and typed.

May 31, 2020

Just in case any of us have forgotten how little the police care about us or the rule of law, I was driving through an intersection when a squad car, stopped at the same intersection, fired up the roof lights and started moving through. As I threw on the brakes to let her pass, she gunned it through the intersection, then immediately slowed down, turned off the roof lights, and just started drifting down the next block as if nothing had happened.

White allies, accomplices and "good cop" friends, these are the sorts of aggressive behaviors that communicate to folx of color that the police are not here to protect us and have no concern for our safety. Even in moments of peace (the curfew hadn't gone up yet), our lives are STILL at risk.

I'm lucky that I'm the type of person of color that society deems nothing, to no one, of no consequence. That's my privilege: that a careless act like this, perpetrated by an officer of the law, is much less likely to get me killed than other non-white ethnicities.

BUT THAT'S NOT A PRIVILEGE. That's still a [W]hite person making choices grounded in ethnicity-based bias that put [B]lack and [B]rown people's lives at risk: in a word, RACISM. #asians4blacklives #blacklivesmatter

Paul is an Episcopal clergy person in training. They graduated from Yale's Master of Divinity Program. Most of their social media posts are an invitation for their friends and followers to engage with the human struggle now and not wait around for the afterlife. This Facebook post received a lot of comments. Some people offered their support, others railed at the system, many shared similar experiences, one or two wondered about the officer's personal issues and one began an exceedingly unproductive rant invalidating the experiences of everyone else in the thread and dismissing their feelings.

Paul attempted to engage the person anyway, trying to find a conversational inroad and inviting more productive dialogue. The attempt wasn't successful. The person shut down, spewing one final derisive comment, then going silent on the issue. A few of Paul's other Facebook friends responded with *Paul, don't waste your time with this person* or *They're not worth it.*

But, as Paul told me during our interview, "I don't consider attempting to engage with anyone a waste of time. Facebook may not be the best medium, but every person deserves kindness and respect. Every person is dealing with some sort of pain."

Paul cares about every human soul and thinks it's important not to vilify individuals as "bad" but rather to acknowledge that, although there are good and bad behaviors, the vast majority of people are inherently decent. This means that, even as a person of color, they feel empathy for those espousing values that perpetrate systems of White supremacy.

"There is a term I got from one of my mentors at Yale, Dr. Linn Tonstad—intellectual violence. We know about emotional and physical violence and the languages and patterns of abuse that exist between a number of identity markers, but the idea of intellectual violence—violating a person's understanding of themselves, when they are presented with a truth that invalidates their world view—is really hard. We are asking people to make changes to behaviors that are tied to their sense of personal, communal and individual identity, and they are being asked to make changes immediately that involve them taking on what they perceive as a lack of privilege. I've met very few people who have participated in some type of armed service where their occupation is not a huge part of who they are. My vocation is a huge part of who I am, and it's decidedly committed to non-violence. My identity as a trans non-binary person of color is a huge part of who I am. When that gets transgressed, that hurts a lot, and it's very hard to reconcile those relationships. I think, if we want healing, those of us who have the emotional capacity to be able to step back and be able to remain in community with people, as opposed to unfriending or unfollowing, or making funny but cruel jokes that dehumanize people rather than systems, have to do the work for other people who are in greater spaces of pain."

Paul isn't saying we shouldn't enforce change—immediately. They are saying that we need to urgently intervene by altering the systems and structures that support and perpetuate all the -isms and -phobias currently impacting society, but these behaviorally-focused intervenetions won't change emotions. That calls for empathy, which requires recognizing our shared humanity.

Paul's position is a mirror image of my own. It's essential to see, hear and acknowledge all people because, if what we're fighting against is lack of recognition, we must model a different way of being.

Across the nation, we are seeing the effects of attempts at the erasure of Asian identity and cultural reclamation. This occurs in the tokenism of the Asian minority population and the underrepresentation of Asians in literature and in film. According to United Nations' statistics, Asians represent close to 60% of the world's population, while the USC Annenberg's 2017 report revealed that out of 1,100 popular films, only 6.3% of actors were of Asian descent. While this 6% number may seem to be reflective of the percentage of Asians in America, it is not at all sufficient, especially given that Asians are seldom cast in lead roles and that, even with movies such as *Crazy Rich Asians*, the actual lives of most people are not being reflected. It's alienating to be consistently overlooked and perpetually foreign. In my research and interviews, I've come across individual narratives of people moving about the world feeling unseen, except when they've been actively othered.

Cinder Kuss told me that they had no real romantic life until they were in college because throughout middle and high school none of their White Jewish peers wanted to have a relationship with someone

Asian—even though Cinder's father was Jewish and Cinder was raised Jewish.

As Don Wyatt, East Asian Studies Director at Middlebury College, explained it, one of the difficulties currently facing Asian Americans is the difficulty of having been categorized as a "model minority." If you're not familiar with this term (which I wasn't until Don shared it with me), it refers to the stereotyping of a particular minority community that simultaneously casts them as other and as exemplary.

You're no doubt familiar with the stereotypes swirling around Asian populations in America—as if every Asian individual is supposed to be studious, small of stature, well-behaved and unobtrusive—an example to which other racial minorities should aspire. If you're thinking *but aren't all of these things good? What's the problem?*, think again. Any conflations that collapse a collection of individuals into a single, homogenous entity is a form of racism that, by stripping an individual of their multidimensionality is, in essence, a form of dehumanization.

Paul Reese has many intersecting identities—musician, academic, clergyperson-in-training, gender non-binary—but the first thing people see when they look at them is that they are Asian. That's what the police officer saw when she cut them off in traffic, just to prove her power and her prowess. Sadly, being Asian in America means that sometimes a person isn't looked at but looked through. It means not being depicted as "dangerous," as with other individuals of color, but of being overlooked as unimportant and inconsequential.

Paul shared that "There are times when I feel like my pain and the pain of other Asians has been eclipsed, but then I remember that the souls of Black folk have been so incredibly oppressed and challenged, crushed for so damn long. My life is less at risk than other folks of color, but it is all part of the same fight. We are talking about different expressions of the same unjust system."

Long before the COVID-19 pandemic, before the Black Lives Matter movement swelled to its current crescendo, before it was trendy, Paul Reese entered into the quest for human liberation. They understood that this was not and is not a fight by minorities against the majority, but, rather, that it is a battle against the systems and the ideologies that are eviscerating everyone—body, mind, and spirit.

(You may remember Paul's earlier inclusion in Chapter 6, p. 70 where I spoke about the book *Dying of Whiteness*).

As Paul explained, their Episcopal vocation is one that mandates that they take action to ensure the physical, mental and emotional wellbeing of their fellow humans before any meaningful spiritual intercession can occur. That means meeting people where they are, which requires acknowledging the current status quo (something many people don't want to look at, because it's hard to confront head-on).

"At least in my work, I'm questioning myself every day," Paul informed me. "What does it mean to be a clergy person in training, and what does it look like to be concerned about the spiritual well-being of someone else? Right now, because we have so much need, in terms of poverty, injustice, racial inequality, ableism, ageism, so many different ways of discrimination based on peoples' identity markers that usually involve problems with housing insecurity or food insecurity then one of the base level things a pastor can do is to help support people in their survival needs because it's very difficult to give a person the space and privilege of spiritual health when they're hungry and cold."

Cinder Kuss knows what it is to be hungry and cold. Their family suffered a temporary period of homelessness and the impact of that has been lifelong. Now that Cinder is an adult, they refuse to knowingly let anyone go without a place to stay. They've offered their couch to strangers.

"Not because I'm an especially good person," they explained. "But, because I've experienced poverty, I want to spare others that pain."

Cinder's struggle for equity is one that goes beyond a desire to help others. It is deeply personal.

"I feel like, in common understanding, advocacy means you are speaking on behalf of someone else and not yourself," they told me. "And I'm certainly out there for Black indigenous people but, also, as an Asian person, I really want a world where anti-Black, anti-indigenous racism doesn't exist, because I believe that will be a better world for me as well. Also, I'm Jewish. This really intense anti-Blackness, Nazism also has its root in anti-Judaism. I criticize White mainstream American Judaism for not recognizing that and not being more involved in this fight."

Ethnically, Cinder is half-Korean, half-Jewish, but they were raised in a home that was culturally Jewish and which attempted to suppress Korean cultural identity and ethnic affinity. "My dad was overtly racist against Korean culture and my mom was totally infatuated with White American society, so they were like our kids should be the least Korean as possible, we're not going to teach them Korean deliberately. We don't want them to have an accent. We don't want people to identify them as Korean. We want them to be Jewish."

Even within their own family, it felt as if their Asianness were being erased and, yet, at the same time, there was a dissonance between what they were told at home and how they were perceived by others. Of their experiences engaging with the White heteronormative majority, Cinder said, "When White people want to oppress me, they'll say I'm Asian. When White people want to rebuff my attempts to shame them, they'll say I'm White. And that's how I know I'm Asian and I'm not White."

Because Asian Americans have historically existed in the straddle space of skin-privilege, many of them have had to grapple with the impact of that. Sometimes, it can cause an internal sense of othering wherein a person feels compelled to strive for Whiteness.

Of their Korean heritage, Cinder told me "I was ashamed of that part of my identity for so long."

Likewise, Jon Quénard, half-White, half-Asian, struggled to embrace his Asian identity for most of his childhood and adolescence.

"I grew up in Switzerland, which was really, really White," he said. "I didn't really notice I was different until I would go visit my grandparents. Everything was super Vietnamese. From everything we ate, to the language in the house, to the Buddhist shrine in the area where we would pray. I remember not feeling comfortable when I was there. I think it was because that environment made me realize that I was different than the other kids at school, and that made me uncomfortable to the point where I unconsciously didn't like Asian food."

Jon described his discomfort at his own perception of his difference as something that stemmed from within, but, as we explored together, it became clear that he was someone who had gotten caught in the model minority trap. Jon grew up in Switzerland and moved to the United States as a teenager. He said he felt special because of that.

"My experience was extremely welcoming. People were super curious about my background, in a really positive way. I was a question mark and they wanted to understand me and ask me questions. There was some sort of positive bias. I definitely felt seen. I felt like I was a piece in a museum."

Being a piece in a museum can make a person feel admired and adored, but it can also feel like a lot of pressure and it can be internalized in such a way that people start to feel like objects.

"The bias that I've experienced is that people think I'm Asian, so I'm smart," he continued. "I've got to be smart, and so I've bought into that and also created a lot of pressure for myself to be quote unquote successful—academically, athletically, and now in my career. It's like not being successful would feel like being a failure, and so that's like kind of like the other end of the spectrum [of prejudice]."

On this two-sided spectrum, one side is tokenism, the other is terror.

Cinder grew up on the terror side, constantly fearful. They were regularly beat up for their Asian identity. Throughout their elementary and middle-school years, high schoolers would jump them on the street, picking on the small, defenseless Asian/Jewish child because there was no one to stop them from enacting their cruelty. Nobody cared enough to intervene.

One of Cinder's most vivid and distressing memories of being attacked is an incident that occurred when they were ten years old. A new kid had moved into the neighborhood and he and Cinder were outside playing when a woman Cinder had never recognized—the child's mother—stormed out of her house and across the street, picked Cinder up, and threw them across the yard. Cinder lay there, stunned, while this grown woman spewed racial epithets.

"That's the first time anyone ever called me a half-breed," they recalled, insinuating that it was not the last. "She told me, 'If I ever catch you near my son again, I'll kill you!'"

Cinder ran inside and told their dad what had happened and their dad called the police who came to their house but did nothing. Cinder's dad did nothing either. Their mother had left the family to live in Korea for a couple of years, and, as Cinder recalled, "My dad had no words for me."

All these years later, Cinder laughs about the incident, but in the way of someone who's been hurt so often there are no more tears. It wasn't until they left home, moved to Philadelphia, and began to embrace their obvious Asianness, that what Cinder described as the process of "breaking intergenerational curses" could begin. Only now, as an adult, are they finding spaces where they feel they have a place. It's far from perfect. "Maybe you can relate as a mixed-race person," they told me, "but knowing where I belong, where I fit in, is like ugh." Cinder sighed. "I hate thinking about it because, most days, it feels like nowhere."

Cinder's very particular struggle of not feeling White enough for his White-Jewish parent and peers and not Korean enough for his Asian ones is one that a lot of mixed-race people experience. In Cinder's case, it has only been in embracing themselves as an Asian person that they have developed an appreciation for their identity as a person of color and discovered a strong internal drive to fight for liberation.

Don Wyatt's story of coming to appreciate the beauty and complexity of Asian cultures is a lot different than Cinder's. Don is African American and was drawn to Asian Studies as an outsider. "I never commenced the study of China with the aim of becoming Chinese," he told me. "I wanted to extract and appreciate and gain a command of the wealth of experiences of the culture."

A lifelong lover of history who believes that studying the past will tell us who we are in the present, the entry point into the Asian diaspora was the written and spoken word.

"I've always had a real passion for literate cultures—people who have written their history down, and I think China's culture is the archetypal example of that. Everything is written down," he told me. "I had studied other languages previously, but I was never as adept with those as I became with Chinese language, beginning with the study of Mandarin."

Don believes that "studying language is a way of reducing barriers. Once you understand how people communicate, you begin to understand how they think."

As someone who has always been a minority—first, as a Black man in America, then as a Black man working in the field of Asian Studies—Don has felt drawn to multicultural alliances between Black diasporic and Asian cultures, but he said it's only recently that he's felt "the stirrings of a kind of awakening" in which Asian Americans are aligning themselves with Black ones, and vice versa.

The division and disconnection that White supremacy perpetuates has left minority groups so splintered off from one another that many minority communities haven't recognized the collective power to effect change that could come from cross-cultural cooperation. That is shifting. And I believe that, as part of that process, we need to dismantle the myths that keep certain populations at a disadvantage, and keep us all divided. Ours is a nation that continues to be defined by partisan politics.

As On-cho Ng, head of the Asian Studies Department at Penn State, pointed out: "Democracy accentuates conflicts and, in fact, modern democracy is based on the notion of 51/49. Think about it: 49%, by virtue of a certain political defeat, becomes a minority."

On-cho was not knocking democracy, and neither am I. There is value to encouraging political participation among all citizens. Nevertheless, it's useful to look at approaches that go beyond the American democratic system to find other models for representation and inclusion. The more we focus on learning from a rich range of intersecting identities and experiences, the easier it becomes to see other people's perspectives.

This ability to look at the world through different lenses is something that Jon Quénard experiences every day, every moment. "It's like having two pairs of glasses. I can put on each set of glasses and see the world that way. I'll put on my White pair of glasses, or my Asian pair of glasses, and it's like I'm understanding parts of each narrative, which makes reconciliation a bit easier."

In the midst of the COVID-19 pandemic, reconciling Whiteness and Asianness can feel like a revolutionary concept. One of the most devastating impacts of COVID-19 has been the rise of anti-Asian sentiment. Since the beginning of the nationwide public-health restrictions, Asians in America have been openly and publicly discriminated against by many individuals, from everyday passersby to the United States President.

And it's not just American Asians.

John Wang, founder of Mastery Academy, was walking down his street, in his neighborhood, in his country of birth, when a random person yelled at him "Go back to your country!"

John is ethnically Taiwanese, Canadian by citizenship. He was in his country. Even if he weren't, what emboldens someone to be so blatantly intolerant of another human being that they would verbally accost them based solely on their physical appearance? John told me that he felt sorry for the man and saw his prejudice as an expression of pain and an inadequate education. Admittedly, part of the reason John could take this stance is that he has money and means, the love and support of family and friends, food security and so many other things that many others don't. Especially now.

A 2020 report by Farrell, Wheat, & Mac from the JPMorgan Chase Institute found that, although Black-owned businesses were the most severely impacted by the COVID-19 pandemic, Asian-owned businesses weren't far behind. Asian business owners reported that their cash balances were down 22% in April and their revenue reduced by more than 60%. With the rise of COVID-19, suddenly, a group of individuals who had been held up as an example of the ideal racial minority were being vilified. Many non-Asian Americans blamed their Asian-American contemporaries for a public health crisis that began on the other side of the world. People stopped ordering Chinese and Japanese food, going to Chinese-owned nail salons, and visiting their Korean acupuncturists.

As Don Wyatt put it, "Whereas many of us are contracting or have the coronavirus, Asian Americans have been vilified in such a way that they are the coronavirus."

The vilification of Asians in America is not without precedent. From the 1882 Chinese Exclusion Act to the World War II internment of approximately 120,000 Japanese Americans (62% of whom were United States citizens), our White supremacist system has a history of othering Asians at times, including them at others, and, mostly, ignoring them altogether.

There are more than 22 million Asian Americans in this country, a number that represents 6% of the population. Six percent that is an essential part of American society. Yet, in the middle of a global pandemic, it was shown, yet again, that Asian Americans' privileged minority status can be taken at any time, as highlighted by the American President referring to COVID-19 as "the Chinese virus" or, perhaps even more offensively, "kung flu."

COVID-19 should have illuminated the reality that we're all interconnected. If a virus could first arise in one part of the world and, within a matter of months, spread to every pocket of humanity, that is evidence that separation is an illusion.

When people began getting sick, everyone had the same basic concerns—the health and wellness of themselves and their loved ones, financial security, and the need to maintain a sense of connection during alienation. Although the virus impacted different communities differently, with higher mortality rates among minorities, the more than 22 million confirmed cases and 777,000 deaths were a sobering reminder that everyone is mortal. The rising number of cases provided indisputable evidence that we are all part of the same human ecosystem.

It's staggering that, even in the face of a global pandemic, instead of seeking opportunities for connection, there were many who used a public health crisis as a way to reinforce difference and division.

Born and raised in Hong Kong, and with a PhD from the University of Hawaii, On-cho's personal and professional exposure to various cultural influences has made him appreciate that all people have equal value. But, in order to see that, a person has to stop dehumanizing those they perceive to be different from themselves. As it happens, dehumanizing anyone dehumanizes everyone. The minute an individual, or collective of individuals, starts saying, "We're inherently better than them" is the minute it starts to not be okay to exhibit even a hint of human weakness.

"As a human person, the besetting sin or evil of racism is the refusal to acknowledge that all humanity is equal, is the same to begin with," On-cho told me. "You construct this idea that other peoples are fundamentally inferior."

Racism is predicated on a false sense of superiority that dehumanizes both the oppressor and the oppressed.

"The work of any reconciliation along the lines of the basis of identity requires vulnerability, a vulnerability that we are told is not of value within the American way of being," Paul Reese pointed out. "There's part of me that wants to say just ignore the American way of being and just try it. The part of me that believes in the work that I'm doing says...that's so hard. It's so hard to share even a little of oneself with another being because there is the possibility of being hurt. I won't claim to understand anyone else's pain because sometimes I can't even understand my own. The work of being present and vulnerable, learning how to tell your story, and learning how to listen, really listen, to someone else's story and accept it for how it is presented to you and let it affect you and change you—I think that's the work we are trying to do."

When I asked Paul which skill they think is the most essential, their reply was unequivocal: "Listening to each other. Unqualified listening is worth talking about, and maybe even trying."

John Wang agreed about the value of listening. "I think one universal principal is that we want to be heard and we want to be seen," he said. "So many of our conflicts stem from that one thing of we want to be heard first, rather than we want to hear first. But, oftentimes, when we accept and we hear the other person and we see their humanity, it makes it easier to connect. Then, we're not talking *at* people. We're talking *with* people. We're connecting with each other."

To listen to someone, you have to first acknowledge that they are worth listening to. Historically, minorities have not been afforded that respect. Their voices have not been centered.

Cinder Kuss doesn't believe in waiting for recognition, or in advocating for it.

"When you advocate for something, it's like you're asking for something from someone who can give it to you," they told me. "And I think that's an oppressive framework to organize from. Liberation is much more powerful."

I had never heard this perspective about advocacy and liberation being different, but my conversation with Cinder inspired me to explore this concept more deeply. Advocacy is offering support for a particular cause or policy whereas liberation is the act of setting someone free from imprisonment or oppression. I don't see these frameworks as mutually exclusive, but I do think that freedom is far more decisive and declarative. I hope that minorities are done waiting to be heard and seen and validated.

Yes, people need to start listening to those who have not been heard. At the same time, patience is overrated. I long for the day when there is enough mainstream recognition of the value of diversity that every person feels seen and heard. But, in the absence of attentive and receptive ears, I hope that those whose voices have been muted will rise up and shout out. I urge more people to join the fight for liberation and to become advocates for themselves and others. We need to break free from the systems of subjugation by seeing others as worthy of respect and recognition.

Visibility is important—not visibility as part of the current systems of supremacy, but visibility that is at once diverse and inclusive.

As John MacDonald, Professor of Criminology and Sociology at the University of Pennsylvania, pointed out "The whole idea of assimilation to help people be successful is not a zero-sum game. You want to maintain some of your cultural identity, because it has real value. Not just psychic value, but social value. There's almost no evidence that, at least for kids, that that's a hindrance to economic outcomes. Kids are quite capable of navigating multiple cultures and doing well in school and speaking a different language at home and respecting multiple languages. There's no evidence that you need to completely assimilate and abandon your culture. If anything, there's the potential that losing some of that culture will mean losing some of the benefits that culture provides."

As long as cultural assimilation remains the goal, there is no way to achieve equality. If you're trying to be something or someone other than your authentic self, there's no way you'll ever succeed. Even if you do, you've erased your identity. But, as Don Wyatt pointed out, White supremacy has a way of making you pick sides.

Racism sets up a false elevation of Whiteness that forces people into two categories: White and non-White. These binary conceptions then further reinforce division by ranking certain people as inferior and others as superior.

Collapsing distinctions between self and others requires collapsing the structures that support supremacy.

"No particular culture has all the answers," Don told me. "There is always some way in which we can profit from exchange and dialogue with cultures other than our own."

It's essential to cultivate an appreciation for multiple cultures, beginning with our own. That's where Cinder Kuss and Jon Quénard are.

"I'm at the point where I'm having fun discovering what being Vietnamese is," Jon said. "I love this part of me."

I hope that people, all people, will one day wake up to the fact that all people have value and people from different parts of the world, different parts of the country, different upbringings, different languages, different backgrounds, etc. have a lot to offer. We can't embrace others from a place of equity and empathy while operating from the vantage point that any one culture possesses all the answers.

One thing I came to learn through my interviews was something Don Wyatt told me about the Chinese view of belonging.

"In China," he said, "cultural definition has never been principally ethnic. It's been the degree to which you can appropriate Chinese cultural values and therefore the Chinese are very accepting in a way of people who are ethnically different but have gone the distance to appropriate their outlook, their value system, and their cultural attributes."

This way of expanding ideas about inclusion by going beyond race and focusing on values offers a conducive framework for inclusion. It's not perfect. Other value systems hold merit, but it might be constructive for mainstream American society to become inviting in this way. Instead of appropriating based on skin color or physical features, what would shift if people assessed their relative compatibility and affinity based on actions and beliefs?

I asked Don how one assesses shared cultural values, which brought our conversation back to the written and spoken word.

"Chinese [people] are always very encouraging, very complimentary, and very impressed by someone who's trying to acquire their language," he told me, which prompted me to ask if he had a favorite phrase or idiom.

He thought for a moment then said "放龙入海(Fàng lóng rùhǎi), which means 'release the dragon into the sea.'" Don went on to explain that the saying can also be translated as "give a person a chance to show what they can do," which is essentially a way of reminding us to give everyone a fair chance at success, judge them by their actions, and assume positive intent.

My hope is that, instead of vilifying, overlooking, or erasing other cultural influences or individuals who, by virtue of their external appearance, have up until now been marked as other, American culture can move from hierarchy to harmony. As On-cho explained it, "Harmony is to collapse as best you can the distinctions between artificial barriers."

Othering is the erection of artificial barriers coupled with the imposition of vertical methods of evaluating history and the deliberate ignorance of horizontal ones. Vulnerability erases such barriers and forces us to confront our most basic humanity. It is from this space that healing can happen.

During the Black Lives Matter protests, Paul Reese worked as a medic, ministering to the sick and suffering. They brought water to soothe the parched throats of protesters, and helped to treat visible injuries and invisible ones. Mostly, they were there to love and to listen. That's what we all need—to feel seen and heard, to be held and supported, and to remain safe enough that our identities have the freedom to soar.

If you have the companion *Demystifying Diversity Workbook*, please turn to the exercises for Chapter 9 and start them. Return to Chapter 10 in this book when you have completed them.

10 Embodiment

"There is something aside from diet culture and trying to control your body. There is a different way of living."

Aaron Flores, registered dietician nutritionist,
Certified Body Trust® Provider

Thanks to his body, Brian Pollack's dreams had come true. Every night and twice a week during the day for Wednesday and Sunday matinees, he'd get to enact his lifelong aspiration. Every step and turn and lift were flawless. The audience was enthralled. Time was both suspended and sped up—two hours flew by. When the show ended, Brian and the others would run out for the curtain call and all the admiring strangers would leap to their feet, clapping and cheering. None of them had ever suspected that, behind Brian's wide smile was a secret, simmering pain. Why would they? They had come to escape, something he could not do.

Brian's feelings about food, weight, and his body had come to feel like the ballet belt he wore during performances. He couldn't escape the confinement or control. He'd agonize over what and how and when and how much to eat, feel guilty if he "overindulged," or swing from semi-starvation to rebellion, subsisting for weeks on only mac and cheese. Yes, it had been his body's strength, agility, and grace that had earned him a role on Broadway. But he'd stopped appreciating it.

Thanks to his body, Brian Pollack's dreams had come true. Every night, and twice a week during the day for the Wednesday and Sunday matinees, he'd get to enact his lifelong aspiration. Every step and turn and lift would be flawless. The audience was enthralled. Time seemed both suspended and sped up as the two hours flew by. When the show ended, Brian and the others would run out for the curtain call and all the admiring strangers would leap to their feet, clapping and cheering. None of them ever suspected that, behind Brian's wide smile was a secret, simmering pain. Why would they? They had come to escape, something he could not do.

Brian's feelings about food, weight, and his own body had come to feel like the ballet belt he wore during every performance. He couldn't escape the confinement or control. He'd agonize over what and how and when and how much to eat, feel guilty if he "overindulged," or swing from semi-starvation to rebellion, subsisting for weeks on only Mac and Cheese. Yes, it had been his body's strength, agility and grace that had earned him a role on Broadway, but he'd long ago stopped appreciating it.

"My peers and I were judged on how we looked," Brian remembered as he recounted his experiences to me. "We were told we were not good enough. We were told we were not the right shape. We were told we'd never surmount, or amount, to anything. It was brutal. And what you learn in that experience is you can no longer accept what those people are judging. It does a number on you. I think the psychology that is required in that field, I couldn't do."

Brian is now a Licensed Clinical Social Worker and the Founder and Clinical Director of Hilltop Behavioral Health, a facility that specializes in treating eating disorders. Broadway was a couple of careers, and a couple of kids, ago. Nevertheless, he can still vividly recall how he'd gone from being in his body to being disconnected from it and how he'd felt he lacked the psychological resilience to continue subsisting in a state of semi-starvation.

Brian told me that most people in his line of work (eating disorder recovery professionals) tend to fit into one of two categories—those who struggled and went through recovery, and those who had not had eating disorders themselves but could empathize with those who did.

"My situation is unique," he said. "Because I'm in the middle."

The fact that body regulation and oppression are so rampant that Brian categorized his experiences of body loathing, mistrust, and food neuroses as "in the middle" (between disordered eating and food neutrality) is a huge cultural red flag. It's for this reason that I wanted to start with his story, because, as a collective, American society is inflicting a tremendous amount of pain on bodies. All bodies. Bodies that have "made it," and bodies that will never "measure up."

No body is immune to scrutiny. Celebrities' faces are emblazoned on the front pages of tabloid magazines and all over the Internet if their weight moves up or down by ten pounds, an estimated 45 million Americans go on a diet every year, and 79% of us report feeling at least some degree of body dissatisfaction. It's little wonder that eating disorders are on the rise, in all populations.

"I always thought that people who had eating disorders were typically really thin White teenagers who were like rich girls in movies and who were all dancers—and I was a dancer—but who were ballerinas. I had this idea of a perfectionist, very attractive teen girl who was mainly focused on not wanting to be fat or losing weight, whereas the actual reality is that eating disorders come in every shape and size, every socioeconomic background, lots of different cultural and racial identities," Dani Adriana, a Fat Activist, Online Content Creator and Peer Support Advocate, told me. "Also, there's a stigma attached to people in larger bodies. People assume that they might be binge eating or overeating—not that I like to use that term—but there's this stigma attached to people in larger bodies, versus people who are quite thin, whereas the experiences I've had (with my own lived experience, but also my community) show that you cannot tell where someone is in their eating disorder journey based on what they look like and weight tells you very little about what kind of behaviors they're exhibiting with food. So, it's much more complex and rich. There's a lot of layers, especially in terms of mental health. Nobody would say depression looks like one particular type of person, or anxiety looks like one particular type of person, but there's a lot of assumptions made on exterior exhibiters of eating disorders that are actually irrelevant because an eating disorder is a mental illness."

External appearance doesn't tell us anything about what another person is doing behind closed doors. I know this firsthand. When I was binging and purging twelve times a day, passing out at work and having to go to the ER for intravenous fluids, I'd get comments all the time about how great I looked. And, in early recovery, as my body was relearning how to digest, I was asked—by numerous people—if I was pregnant.

When we evaluate one another and ourselves based on external appearance, we are dooming ourselves to existing in the inescapable prison of objectification.

"It was easier for me to unpack diet culture," Dani told me, "because it got to the point where, even if I played the game, I couldn't do it anymore."

Dani never looked like the sick and starving anorexic or the bleary-eyed, bloody-knuckled bulimics she'd imagined, but her eating disorder was no less severe. It was acknowledging this that allowed her to get the help she needed, even if she didn't fit her own stereotypical picture of a person with an eating disorder. These mental constructions about fatness, thinness, and all the judgments we superimpose on bodies is a widespread perpetration of systems of subjugation and suppression. It's not helping anybody and, in fact, it's hurting all of us.

"We live in a world that is hyper-focused on bodies—which bodies fit, which bodies don't, which bodies are fit, which bodies aren't, which bodies belong, which bodies don't. There's all these binaries around bodies," Jennifer Kreatsoulas, PhD, certified yoga therapist specializing in eating disorders and body image, told me. "If we could all just shift the focus from the external body to the stuff of the internal, that would make the world a more comfortable place for all bodies. I can't even tell you how many times I hear people mindlessly standing in line at the grocery store, turning to someone and shaming themselves for the food in their cart, or talking about their diet. Eliminating the morality language around food and our bodies. Let's start there. Food isn't good or bad. Food is neutral. Food is food."

It's taken a long time and a lot of inner work for Jennifer to embrace the idea of food neutrality. She had to first embark on her own recovery journey before she could achieve liberation around food and weight and body. She was one of the lucky ones.

According to the National Association of Anorexia Nervosa and Associated Disorders (ANAD), "at least 30 million people of all ages and genders suffer from an eating disorder in the US." The current United States population, as reported by the US and World population clock, is approximately 330 million. That means that 9% of those living in this country engage in one or more of the following behaviors: binging, purging, starving, exercising to the point of physical, mental and emotional exhaustion, taking handfuls of laxatives and doing things with food and movement that severely impede their ability to show up for life. This 9% doesn't include people whose disordered eating doesn't rise to the level of severity to be labeled an eating disorder but nevertheless are caught in the trap of diet culture and body hatred. And it doesn't include the 70% of Americans who have been labeled by modern medicine, culture and the media as "overweight" or "obese." I put those two words in quotes because that's not language I personally choose to use to describe larger bodies. In fact, in my opinion, those words ought to be categorized as hate speech due to the psychological trauma they inflict.

Fat phobia in America is rampant. It's also a type of prejudice that is socially endorsed and reinforced in a myriad of subtle and overt ways. According to Psychology Today, research reveals that over 50% of doctors described their fat patients as "ugly, awkward, and non-compliant," one-quarter of nurses reported feeling repulsed by their fat patients, and fat defendants are more likely to receive guilty verdicts than their slender counterparts. Even young children are reluctant to make friends with their larger-bodied peers, which can only stem from the messages they're learning at home, on the playground, or from the nearly 30% of teachers who believe that getting fat is "the worst thing that can happen to someone."

Ours is a culture that worships at the altar of thinness. But what are we worshipping? The results of starvation?

Jennifer and I spoke about how, in the early stages of our respective eating disorders, we received a lot of external validation and positive reinforcement.

"You know," she said, "everywhere I went, I got compliments on how great I looked and how thin I looked. That was very reinforcing, so I kept going with it."

Jennifer's eating disorder began in college, when she was on the crew team.

"I can vividly remember sitting in the boat of eight, all of us sophomore women in college, and our coach making a comment to the effect of 'I can tell how hard you work by how your body changes.' And, for someone like me, who was a perfectionist, a people pleaser, an approval seeker, someone who always prided herself on trying to be the best possible teammate, the way I received those words pushed some buttons inside of me and challenged me to have to prove myself through my external body. Whereas, before that, I was just using my body to have fun, to be a part of a team, to do something I enjoyed. Now, I needed to prove myself by changing my body. And, so, in my effort to show him how committed I was to the team, I started shrinking."

I know what it feels like to shrink. When I was in college, playing Division II volleyball, I got down to ninety-something pounds and my doctor threatened to admit me to a psychiatric hospital. Although I would eventually be admitted to inpatient treatment 18 times within roughly a decade, at 17, I had not yet begun that revolving-door process. I was terrified at the prospect of going inpatient. More terrified of that than of gaining weight. I begged my doctor to let me try to weight-restore on my own. He agreed to suspend inpatient for a few weeks, provided the number on the scale was considerably higher the next time I came in for an appointment. I saw him just before school let out for Winter Break and, as soon as I returned from college to Connecticut, I started nonstop binging. I gained 30 pounds in a month, hit my desired weight, then transitioned to bulimia. For years, I binged and purged daily, yet, despite the torture, shame and secrecy, so many people told me I looked healthy, vibrant and beautiful that I lost count. They said things like "You have the perfect body" and "I wish I could look like you." I hated what I was doing to my body but I couldn't stop and, to make matters worse, I was receiving positive reinforcement for starving, stuffing myself full of food, throwing up, and taking handfuls of laxatives. We can't tell from another person's external appearance what they're doing with food and, even if we could, we should be focused on encouraging self-respect and empowerment, rather than some arbitrary, and ever-changing concept of body uniformity.

"I want to bring awareness to the truth that eating disorders come in all shapes," Jennifer told me. "We tend to think of eating disorders as looking one specific way, affecting one specific group. The thin, moving towards emaciated, White adolescent, middle to upper class girl. Not that that segment is not a significant portion of the eating disorder population, but it's only a segment."

Just as there are many different forms bodies can take, eating disordered or not, there are a lot of intersecting and complex factors that cause and contribute to the development of how we behave with food.

"These are biologically-based disorders and I think sometimes we forget that and we get into stigmatization and judgment and avoidance of others," Brian told me. "If you are someone whose DNA has a propensity, it is more likely to get triggered and our society is putting more and more pressure on people. We need to look at the intersection of culture and self and body."

The more we try to control bodies (other people's and our own) the more we trigger patterns of control and rebellion. Food ceases to become neutral and becomes nuclear. It takes on the power to explode and implode our lives. It is incumbent upon all of us to see body regulation as an expression of supremacy and subjugation and to wake up to the fact that the widespread policing of bodies is another form of systemic oppression. As it is, the majority of Americans don't seem to recognize that fat-bodied people are people.

Sixty-one percent of Americans see nothing wrong with making negative remarks about a person's weight, even going so far as to publicly shame others based on the shape and size of their body.

Emily Zargan knows this firsthand. Emily and I are comedy improv acquaintances. We've laughed together and shared a stage, but, until recently, we'd never spoken about weight stigma or body insecurity. It's not something people typically talk about. It can be difficult to be open about weight stigmatization, but it's also healing.

Then, on June 29th, 2020, I saw a post on Facebook in which Emily recounted an experience that prompted me to reach out to her. I sent a private message to see if she'd be willing to be interviewed.

She replied immediately. Absoluuuuuuutely. I feel that fat voices (for a complete lack of a more poetic way to phrase it) are so unheard— we're often met with judgment or disbelief about what we have to say or what we've experienced. And yeah, what happened was shitty. But it's not creative or new.

A few days later, Emily told me the full version of the story that she had briefly shared on social media:

She was at home quarantining with her fiancé and her family when she began scrolling through Facebook posts and noticed that, on the page of her former yoga studio, the owners had posted a message saying that wearing a mask was hazardous to one's health. This was Emily's community yoga studio. Before it shut its doors for good, she could see it from her bedroom window. Her fellow yogis lived in and around her community. Many of them were friends. Although Emily isn't typically one to engage in discussions via social media about public or political issues, she thought it was important to raise awareness within her local community. She wrote a well-reasoned response to the anti-mask message, laying out a point-by-point explanation about why it was and is important to adhere to Center for Disease Control (CDC) guidelines and how doing so is ultimately health-supporting for individuals and for society at large. That was when Laura, a fellow follower of the studio's page, bashed Emily for her body shape, telling her that taking health advice from her would be ludicrous and heavily insinuating that she should go and stuff her face full of muffins.

Sadly, the most devastating part of Emily's narrative wasn't what Laura did or said. It was the fact that Emily described the experience as something that had happened before and would happen again.

"I don't have the mental rent to be upset with her. I'm 28 years old and this is absolutely not the first time it's happened. I think the first time it happened I was in the fourth grade. This is something I've been dealing with my whole life."

In our diet-obsessed culture, once a person's body lies outside some subjective idea of what's considered desirable, it's as if their value as a human is diminished. And this devaluation only becomes compounded because so many of us internalize it. We swallow the delusions of diet-culture and then shame ourselves for our shape and size or what we choose to eat.

How many times have you heard someone say something to the effect of "I was so bad. I ate ice cream" or "I was so good. All I had was a salad"? How many times have you been the one to make these types of comments?

Judgments around food and body feed into the shame and stigma that has led to pervasive body dissatisfaction and are destructive. When culture tells people that the worst thing in the world is to be fat, it's little wonder we have a rising epidemic of bulimia, binge eating disorder, and anorexia. Anorexia has the highest fatality rate of any mental health malady. It is estimated that 4% of anorexics will die from complications of the disease.

Bibi Lorenzetti said of herself when she was actively anorexic, "I stopped seeing myself for who I was. When I would look in the mirror, it was almost like I couldn't recognize the image of me that I had in my mind, or that I should be. What I would see didn't match the idea that I had of the ideal me. These were all mental constructions that I created. The ideal me kept shifting to something smaller and smaller and smaller."

Body dysmorphia occurs in most anorexics, but it is not confined to the anorexic population. It exists on a spectrum of inaccurate self-perception. Within diet culture, we are all operating inside an unfun fun house, our images of ourselves distorted. Brian told me that, in his practice, although some men suffer from the anorexic drive for thinness, what he's seeing among most of his male clients is what he referred to as "the drive for muscularity that is part of the masculine mystique of what it is to be a man in our culture."

The psychological violence that is oppressing bodies afflicts each and every one of us and it's a zero-sum game. Even when we win, we lose.

As Aaron Flores, registered dietician and certified Body Trust Provider, told me, "I'm both shocked and saddened when I see celebrities saying 'Here's what I eat in a day.' They are basically talking about and glorifying their eating disorder. Every minute of their life is dictated by what they will eat, what they won't eat, and when they'll exercise."

We need to rethink societal expectations around bodies and to seek liberation rather than arbitrary ideals. This means evolving beyond seeing our bodies as objects to be controlled and manipulated and, instead, connecting with our sensory perceptions and becoming awakened to the reality that our bodies are the vehicle through which we experience life. This isn't the same as going from hating what our bodies look like to loving how they look. It's much deeper and more complex than that. The more we focus on bodies as objects, whether we are criticizing or admiring them, the more we are perpetuating the same cycles.

As Dani put it, "If you've gone to body positivity just to feel beautiful, it's just going to give you that same empty feeling."

Ranking our bodies according to some imaginary ladder of superiority and inferiority keeps us from developing our intuitions and becoming free to do what works for us in terms of food and movement. Instead of thinking about your body as beautiful or ugly or any other descriptive adjective, I encourage you to focus instead on its physical sensations. To inhabit your body instead of oppressing it. I don't mean to suggest that this is an easy or linear process. You don't just snap the fingers in your mind and dispense with decades of diet-culture indoctrination. I got out of my last inpatient treatment center at the end of 2009. It's been 11 years. Yet, there are days, or even weeks, when I feel uncomfortable in my own skin—especially when I have an interpersonal interaction that makes me hyper-conscious of my body. I had one recently.

I live in an apartment complex in Mt. Airy, PA, a Philadelphia suburb. Mt. Airy is a diverse and welcoming place. Signs on front yards read: *Kindness is everything. Science is real. Black lives matter. Love is love. Diversity is celebrated. Hate is voluntary. It's not fake news. No human is illegal. I support the Paris Agreement. Women's rights are human rights. Religious freedom for everyone. Power of love > love of power. Climate change is not a hoax. Resist. Persist. Coexist.*

People say hello to each other. They care. My apartment building feels like an extension of that. Neighbors stop and chat with one another in the hall. We ask "How are you doing?" then slow down long enough to listen to the other person's answer. Every resident is on a first name basis with the building maintenance man, who I'll refer to as Norman.

I'd just gotten home from running errands when I spotted Norman standing in the courtyard. We exchanged our typical hellos, a few pleasantries, and our respective observations about the beauty of the weather and the ugliness of the world.

As I was getting ready to say goodbye and head inside, Norman spread his arms wide and nodded at me in a gesture that I couldn't quite decipher. "COVID, huh?"

I stared at him, blank-faced, through my Wonder Woman mask. "Pardon?"

Norman repeated the gesture, this time adding "You've really gained weight since all this started."

My reply was reflexive. I didn't think about how to best express my sense of violation at having someone remark about the size of my body.

"Wow. That was rude."

I wasn't willing, in that moment, to engage so instead of sticking around for a discussion, I went inside the building, entered my apartment, and closed the door. Then, I processed what had happened.

Although I don't own a scale and have not weighed myself or been weighed by anyone else (including my doctor) in a decade (because I believe that the only valid measurement regarding my body is how I feel physically, mentally and emotionally) I knew that Norman's assessment was accurate. During the pandemic, my body had expanded. My pants no longer fit and I felt different. Nevertheless, as much as I didn't, and still don't, appreciate anyone commenting on my body, Norman hadn't made any positive or negative assessment about the weight gain. He'd only remarked on it. I had to admit (to myself, if to no one else) that I wouldn't have been offended if he'd said I lost weight. It was painful in that moment to be confronted with my own bias.

As much work as I have done to move beyond anorexia and bulimia, and to recognize that my ability to make meaningful contributions to the world has no relationship to my curves and/or concavities, I still have internalized beliefs about how my body "should" be. This is unsurprising considering I'll be 37 years old in September 2020 and have spent all those years existing in a society where bodies are oppressed and roughly 15 years living in a body that was besieged by active anorexia and bulimia.

I sat down in my plush green Papasan chair and reminded myself of the fact that my inner experience doesn't have to be defined by my externals. I forgave Norman his insensitivity, forgave myself for my interpretation, and took a moment to appreciate that I have moved out of active self-destruction into imperfect, ever-evolving recovery. While I strive for neutrality, some days, I love my body, others, I hate it.

Bibi could relate. "The other day," she told me, her voice infused with laughter, "I was in the bathroom and I had this moment where I looked at my body and I was like *I don't care that it's ten pounds heavier. I love it.* I walked out and went into the kitchen and I told my boyfriend 'I just had this realization… I don't care about shedding the ten pounds. I feel really feminine and really positive, and really beautiful. I'm not worried about it anymore.' And he was like 'Oh that's great.' The next morning, I woke up and I was like 'I hate this!'"

The way we perceive our bodies is subjective. The way we perceive other people's bodies is subjective.

At the risk of belaboring the point, you can't be judging a body and also, be fully alive within it. This means that to experience liberation we have to step outside of diet culture and let go of the mythology that thinness equals happiness. Instead, let's strive to nourish ourselves—physically, mentally, emotionally, and spiritually.

Refocusing our attention away from diet culture can be a scary proposition. Of his work with his clients, Aaron said, "I'm asking them to do something really brave and that is to release the dogma of diet culture and this notion that your body is broken and actually flip it on its head and say your body is not broken. It has a ton of wisdom. Let's tap into that wisdom."

It's true. Our bodies are miraculous. They bring us pleasure and pain. They have internal mechanisms for cellular regeneration, detoxification and healing. We can literally use them to create and grow other lives.

For Bibi, becoming pregnant and giving birth to her now infant child felt like a testament to her recovery and made her feel capable, resilient and unstoppable.

Jennifer had a different experience. "For me, giving birth was extremely traumatic. It was a very specific moment of re-entry into the eating disorder. It's almost embarrassing to share, and I pray that no one judges me, but my relapse started within minutes of giving birth to my second daughter. I didn't know how else to cope. But it didn't cancel out how much I love my daughter, or how much I wanted to bring her into this world. That's what was so hard for me to negotiate with myself. I remember being in treatment and talking about it. I kept asking myself: How do you make sense of loving another human being so much, the human being that you brought into the world, and at the same time feeling so incredibly overwhelmed and not sure how to cope that you start to starve yourself? How do you make sense of that?"

Bibi and Jennifer's experiences help illuminate the reality that there is no one response to the same set of stimuli. Every individual experiences life differently. Everybody filters and interprets the world in unique ways. When it comes to recovery, however, there is something that does seem to be universal. To break free of disordered eating and to step into the space of true body liberation, we have to tap into a source of motivation that is bigger than the allure of fitting into our skinny jeans.

Caitie Corradino, MS, RDN, CDN, RYT told me that, in working with her clients, she asks them to think about their authentic and deeply held values, specifically asking them to think about what they want to be remembered for and the impact they want to make in the world. She invariably finds that people want to love and be loved, to make a positive impact, and so many other things—things they can do at a size two, a size thirty-two, or any size imaginable.

Jennifer valued family and motherhood and it was connecting with those values that enabled her to do the work required to free herself from the hell of an active eating disorder. On Mother's Day 2014, she and her husband and their two kids went to a park and she described it as "there was all this life around me and inside I was dying. I was pushing the youngest in the stroller and I reached a point I couldn't push the stroller anymore. I was too weak. I slumped over the stroller and looked up at my husband and there was this knowing. I thought *This is not fair to my family. This is not the mother I want to be. This is not the wife I want to be. This is not the human being I want to be. And I can't pretend this isn't a problem anymore.*"

She described her path to body liberation as an ongoing and ever-evolving process. Caitie described herself as recovered. My own personal experience of recovery is that it's different, depending on the day, the moment, and the meal. Sometimes, I feel like it's past. Others, it is all too present.

Eating disorder recovery is personal. For some, it's private. For others, it can be both public and symbolic.

Aaron told me "Recovering from an eating disorder or rejecting diet culture and recovering into a larger body is an act of rebellion. With your body, you're making a statement that this is my healing. This body is actually nourished. This body is healed. This body is healthier than the one that was being starved. I think this is where the social justice lens comes in. Personally, I don't choose words like *body positivity* for a couple of reasons. For one, it's been co-opted by a lot of big companies and a lot of diet companies. Further, when I put in that hashtag on my social media, I don't see any diversity in that image. I see a lot of thin White women who are showing off their rolls in their yoga pants, mid pose. That's, to me, not body positivity. I want to see someone who looks like me. I want to see large bodies, small bodies, I want to see people of color. I want to see trans bodies, non-binary bodies. I want to see bodies that are disabled. I want to see able bodies.

I want to see diverse representation. Often, *body acceptance* is not great language either. For trans folks, body acceptance is a term that could imply *you want me to accept the body I'm in that doesn't align with my gender or how I see myself. I can't accept that. I'm going to work on changing my body.* And there are a lot of very challenging acceptance issues for bodies that are dealing with chronic pain. Neutrality is hard for me too, because there is so much oppression around bodies. I can't be neutral about it. I'm going to take a stand."

Taking a stand against body oppression is something we can all do every day, without exception. We can engage in small forms of interpersonal freedom by ordering what we want off the menu and refusing to feel guilty about our choices or throwing out our Spanx. Or we can go a few steps further, calling people out when they comment on the size and shape of bodies, or even doing large-scale social justice work. I believe that body liberation is lifelong work that has to begin at the level of the individual before they can join larger conversations around body liberation for all.

As Dani, who frames her eating disorder recovery and her advocacy as an "ongoing check-in" told me, "Knowing that I have a predisposition to want to control things that I can control, which food is one of the biggest things, it's something that I'll probably deal with for the rest of my life. However, I do consider myself in a highly-recovered place." It is from this highly-recovered place that she is able to work to bring greater appreciation for the bodies of others, an appreciation she believes we can start to cultivate with better representation. "The more you see inclusivity and the more you see bodies that look completely different from yours, the more you open your eyes to the fact that bodies are so, so, so diverse—more than we could ever imagine—the easier for us to feel like we fit because suddenly there are no more options. The options are gone and you're allowed to just exist."

Likewise, Aaron believes that seeing diverse bodies living full and free and joyful lives is essential to advancing the freedom and beauty of Health at Every Size to people who are suffering from oppression and objectification.

Brian, who reported being less-than-optimistic about the efficacy of social justice work because of the all-pervasive nature of body oppression, emphasized individual agency and autonomy, because that's something anyone can access within themselves, whether the external world ever shifts.

Of the current culture, he said "It can be beautiful and amazing and wonderful to be an outsider because then you don't have to live in the norms that people think are powerful. You get to build the life you want. You get to be the person you want without having to live within those puppeteered strings of society that we don't feel good about internally."

Brian now has two sons, a three-year-old and a six-year-old. He told me that, one day, his six-year-old came home and announced, "Daddy, you're fat!"

Brian, shocked, took a moment, asked his son to repeat himself, and when he realized that he had, in fact, heard his child correctly, crouched down to his level. He kept his tone calm and inviting when he asked, "Where did you hear that?"

"I heard it from my friends," his son replied. The six-year-old had no way of knowing that what he'd said could be construed as insulting or insensitive and Brian patiently explained that some of the most beautiful, incredible, intelligent people he knows could be described as "fat" and that using that word to describe them, or anyone, could be hurtful.

"You know," he reflected after describing this interaction. "I have never heard him say that word again."

My hope is that we can all take the time to slow down long enough to recognize the impact of judging bodies—our own bodies and other people's bodies. I wish that each and every human had the freedom to let go of external rules and live a more embodied existence. Most of all, I hope that, once we start to practice greater individual liberation, we can educate and inform those around us so that we can all exist squarely in the middle of freedom.

If you have the companion *Demystifying Diversity Workbook*, please turn to the exercises for Chapter 10 and start them. Return to Chapter 11 in this book when you have completed them.

11 Coming Out of the Shadows through Community

> "The importance of immigration in this country is huge. We are all the result of different immigration waves and it's saddening that there is a part of public opinion in the U.S. who thinks of immigration as a threat, when, in fact, as an immigrant, I can say that we bring so much that is new—new points of perspective, new ethics of work, new standards, new cultures, and so on and so on and so on. So, it's saddening when people rally against immigration."
>
> Tulia Falleti, Director of the Latin American and Latinx Studies Program at UPenn

Twelve-year-old Dulce looked around the locked, cramped cage. The only familiar faces were those of her younger brother and older sister. They too searched the space, hoping for a glimpse of their mother. It had been an hour since she had been taken away by the same men who had locked the three adolescents in a cage, barked at them in English, then disappeared without explanation.

What was happening to their mother? Would she be back?

The children didn't speak English. The strangers surrounding them, in their cage and the other adjacent ones, didn't either. The officers hadn't spoken Spanish and, even if they had, they had no interest in listening to the concerns or answering the questions of those they'd deemed "illegal" and "alien."

Dulce and her siblings moved closer together, their bodies casting overlapping shadows on the concrete floor below them. They'd known even before attempting to cross the border that they might be apprehended. They'd been warned about the detention centers. But, in Mexico, they didn't have money for basic necessities, and they missed their father.

Dulce's dad had preceded his family to the United States and had been sending money back at every opportunity. When they spoke on the phone, he told them about how much better conditions were in Philadelphia than in Mexico. Children could go to school for free and, even though he was being paid at a lower rate than if he'd had documents, he was confident that he and his family could advance in America in ways that would not be possible in Mexico.

Reconnecting had become the family's guiding light, leading their actions even in the darkest of days. Dulce, her siblings, and their mother had gotten rid of everything they'd owned—not that they'd owned much—packed all their remaining belongings into a single backpack each and traveled to the border between Mexico and Arizona, where they'd been apprehended.

"When we were arrested, we were taken in a van to a detention center," Dulce recalled. "From there, they had people in what looked like cages outside—because they didn't have enough room to keep them all inside. Sometimes, they even stayed in cages overnight. In the detention centers, we were put in a room, or a cage, with other people. They took my mom to another room. The first time, we thought she was going to be taken away and we were not ever going to see her again."

After their first unsuccessful attempt, Dulce, her two siblings and their mother tried six more times to cross into the United States. Six more times, they risked their safety to escape the ravages of poverty and an inadequate educational system. On three occasions, they were arrested. On three others, their mother had perceived danger, so they'd turned around of their own volition and waited for the next opportunity. It was opportunity that was compelling them to travel to an unknown country with nothing but a few belongings and a desire for a better life.

"It was very difficult for low-income people, like us, to be able to survive in Mexico," Dulce told me. "Even though my dad left as an undocumented immigrant, and of course he didn't get paid the same as a citizen, he was able to provide more for us living and working in Philadelphia than he ever could when he was back in Mexico. He would send money every time he got a paycheck."

The money helped a little, but not enough. Dulce's mother and father agreed that they needed to equip their children with the resources to increase their own earning potential. School in Mexico was precarious. In fact, Dulce told me that the ages of the kids in her grade varied considerably because many children had had to drop out due to lack of funds for tuition and school supplies. They might leave for six months or a year before returning again–if they ever returned at all–impeding advancement.

Had they remained in Mexico, there would have been almost no way to climb out of poverty. The parents wanted more for their children, even if that required them to face fear, uncertainty and danger.

"These were sacrifices we had to make so we could have a better life," Dulce recounted.

It took the four of them—Dulce, her mother, and her two siblings—seven attempts to cross from Mexico into Arizona. After they made it, they had a five-day car ride before reaching their father in Philadelphia. Even when they finally made it to their intended destination, things weren't easy or safe. Their ability to progress continued to be hindered by a nation that, although built by immigrant labor and innovation, has labeled so many who come in search of opportunities for upward social mobility "illegal aliens." This is counter to the approach we ought to take, considering the value Latinx immigrants and other immigrant populations bring to this country when they decide to relocate to the United States.

"Often immigrants will bring entrepreneurship and new businesses," John MacDonald, Professor of Criminology and Sociology at the University of Pennsylvania, told me. "If we want to figure out how to rebirth and revitalize the American economy, one of the best ways would be to encourage immigrants to move to underdeveloped or distressed communities and invest in these places where we're not producing a lot of new populations and where the current generations are declining. Rebuilding communities relies on and requires immigrants."

Whether they worked as day-laborers, doctoral researchers, or something in between those two educational and employment extremes, every person I spoke to who immigrated to the U.S. did so not only to pursue their personal advancement but so that they could more fully contribute to the social collective.

Establishing community and participating in cooperative social networks takes on a special significance when a person is in an unfamiliar place—possibly even a place where they don't understand the predominant language.

"What we have discovered is that, when you are alone as an immigrant and you don't have a community around you, that isolation makes you feel really sad and powerless, but when you have a community around you, you feel empowered," Obed Arango, MSSP, a professor at the University of Pennsylvania, the Founder and Executive Director of the Centro de Cultura, Arte, Trabajo y Educación (CCATE), a Mexican journalist, anthropologist, visual artist, and filmmaker told me.

There is much that can be gleaned, and a great deal of value that can be derived, by looking at immigrant populations as an example of how to simultaneously embrace individuals and the collective.

Sulafa Grijalva is a 23-year-old law school student who, in whatever limited free time she has, volunteers for a mutual aid network and participates in community organizing initiatives.

"I left Ecuador when I was ten," she told me. "My family, my mom and dad, migrated to Canada looking for work because things were not stable at home. That was when I first became a foreigner in a North American country. We were applying for refugee status, but, four years later, it got denied. Things became unstable. My parents also got separated around that time and we all had to be deported to Ecuador. Luckily, we only went back for about two years. And, within those two years, my sister, who was an American citizen, was able to petition for our mom, and consequently me, to come and join her in America. So I came to the States when I was sixteen."

Sulafa attributes her unwavering desire to help those for whom the path to progress has not been paved with privilege on her personal experiences. "I don't know if I would have the same level of passion and empathy about activism and the immigrant community and housing justice as I do, had I not experienced deportation, or had my mom and I not experienced living in a shelter. I know how valuable housing security is because, at one point, I didn't have it."

Studies suggest that immigrants to the United States are much more likely to contribute to the uplifting of others than those who have not had to work to acclimate themselves to American society. As John MacDonald pointed out, "Immigrant enclaves actually generate social capital in the sense that people are more cooperative when they live with each other. There are generally higher levels of volunteerism, which may seem counterintuitive given people's economic circumstances. Yet, they are willing to do things for each other. Neighbors are more willing to watch each other's kids. Part of that is altruistic, and part is likely cultural. The whole idea of assimilation to help people be successful, it's not a zero-sum game. You want to maintain some of your cultural traditions and practices because these things have real value—not just psychic value but social value."

There is a lot that we can learn by looking to the examples of Latinx immigrant networks of support and borrowing from organizational models that emphasize community.

As Obed told me, "I cannot liberate myself. I need my community. Without community, nobody can really liberate him, her, or themselves."

Whether someone is coming to a new country and becoming acclimated to different surroundings and an unfamiliar society, community is essential. Because of this, it is incumbent upon all of us to acknowledge the simultaneous value of others and ourselves. We have to become invested in the upward social mobility and liberation of everyone not through selfish individualism but by cooperation and collaboration.

Our nation has historically emphasized the individual over the collective and we are seeing the results of that type of "me versus the world" thinking.

Tulia Falleti, Ph.D., Class of 1965 Endowed Term Professor of Political Science, Director of the Latin American and Latino Studies Program, and Senior Fellow of the Leonard Davis Institute for Health Economics at the University of Pennsylvania, told me "What I've been seeing in the U.S. is that it's becoming more and more of a third-world country. More and more inequality—high, high, high, very, very high levels of income inequality and inequality of opportunities."

If we want to reverse these disparities in opportunities and income, we have to put less emphasis on individual sovereignty and more on social mobility for all. We have to stop pretending that each individual is an island and instead see every person as part of an interrelated human ecosystem.

There are a lot of intersecting factors conspiring to stifle the upward social mobility of many people living and working in the United States today, people whose contributions are of direct benefit to the American economy and can inspire if, instead of casting immigrants into shadows, we examine and admire—in the light—the stories and the successes of those who find the interpersonal and intrapersonal resources to advance against all odds and even in the seeming absence of agency. Immigrant populations have proven, over and over again, that although many are not documented, they are determined.

John MacDonald told me "There's tremendous self-selection in who becomes an immigrant. It's a difficult process to immigrate to the U.S.—legally or illegally. I mean, you have to leave family. There's often a long journey of thousands of miles. People have to be highly motivated to immigrate, and that means the U.S. benefits from immigrants who come who are highly motivated. They're coming looking for economic opportunities. Most people in the U.S. today are descendants of immigrants who came for the same reasons."

An expert in sociology and criminology, John has spent a significant portion of his career focusing on the various factors that contribute to human criminality and has discovered through his research that immigrants have a very low propensity for crime.

"It's called the protective effect of immigration. And there is also something I call the immigrant enclave effect. What I mean by that is, people tend to select places where there are other people of similar backgrounds as them. And often those areas generate thriving economic opportunities through entrepreneurship. People who come and live in those communities have a better chance of getting a job. But it's not just jobs. It's also the social network—knowing how to get resources for your kids, making friends, developing social connections, and ties adds a lot of value."

John told me that there is no basis for the political rhetoric that we saw advanced by Donald Trump during his run for office and throughout his presidency (especially with the emphasis on building a wall and the widespread detainment, arrest, and separation of immigrant families) conflating criminality and immigration. In fact, immigration is correlated with a positive effect on crime rates. John even cited studies that show a 30-40% reduction in serious violent crime with the influx of immigration, thereby demonstrating that, for the vast majority of immigrants coming to this country, the focus is not on crime, but on contribution.

I wondered aloud about pettier violations. By virtue of the fact that undocumented immigrants are prohibited from getting licenses and obtaining work permits, I assumed that many might get caught in the criminal justice system for relatively insignificant and avoidable violations.

"If someone comes here, maybe fleeing political persecution, or poverty, and enters into the U.S. undocumented, by virtue of their status, they can't get a drivers' license. If they get in trouble for that, won't they get caught up in the cycle of criminality?" I asked. "Even if, in many cases, they would have done things the legal way if they had been afforded the opportunity. "

"That's a real challenge," John acknowledged. "But it is pretty amazing how that doesn't happen more. People figure out how to navigate things, even with all these hardships."

Obed told me that those who figure out how to navigate their hardships tend to do so by adhering to much more rigid standards than the rest of us. "We have to be perfect people," he said.

Perfect, unobtrusive, and invisible.

Both Juan Rosa and Juliana Cabrales, the Northeast Director of Civic Engagement and Mid-Atlantic Director for NALEO Educational Fund, respectively, told me that many members of the Latinx community have been fearful about filling out the U.S. census because they are worried about making their whereabouts and identities visible to authorities. There is a lot of fear in immigrant communities because of how they have been dehumanized and discounted by the government and depicted in the media.

Dulce's family, for example, was terrified. After reuniting in Philadelphia, the family of five lived in a tiny studio apartment. "It was a little room and we shared a kitchen and bathroom with another family," Dulce remembered. "It was about three months before my father was able to find an apartment, a two-bedroom apartment, for us to move into." These two apartments were pretty much all Dulce and her siblings saw of the States until they enrolled in school in September.

"We were told not to go outside by ourselves and to be careful with the police because we didn't want to get in trouble and get deported.

So, we arrived in May and we spent all of May until September indoors while our parents worked."

As stifling as it was to be stuck indoors for an entire summer, Dulce was initially trepidatious about the prospect of starting school. She worried that, because her only exposure to English had been four months of watching television and listening to the English-language learning CDs her dad bought them, she wouldn't be able to converse with her peers.

"But," she told me, "when our father brought me and my sister to enroll, the school told us that most of the other kids spoke Spanish and then I was excited to make friends."

"That's great!" I replied.

Up until that point, Dulce's story had been one of perpetual struggle and I wanted her to have found a sense of community and connection. I was invested not only because it's difficult not to care about someone when they're entrusting you with their story, but because to meet Dulce is to love her instantly. The petite young mother has a wide, flashing smile that radiates all the way upward into her eyes, a self-deprecating sense of humor, and a kindness that can't be taught. She is an incredible woman—brilliant, friendly, dynamic, and resourceful. Her character and spirit are what made me ask her for an on-the-record interview. I'd met her previously while on a journalistic assignment. I'd been writing about Vidas Suspendidas, an exhibition highlighting Latinx artists from across Philadelphia.

"I'm glad you had kids your own age who spoke Spanish, too," I said. "Tell me about your first friend."

There was a long pause.

"Well," Dulce said after a while, "I didn't make any friends. My classmates would make racist comments about Mexicans and, also, the way I looked, which was slightly different than them. They'd make fun of the way I spoke. Even though they spoke Spanish, their vocabulary was different."

Apparently, Dulce's Latinx contemporaries were from countries other than Mexico and, instead of focusing on what they had in common, they ridiculed her based on their perception that she was different and, therefore, not as good.

Being made fun of, rejected, and left out at school isn't unheard of for any student, regardless of race, ethnicity, gender, country of origin or any other identity markers. According to the American Academy of Child and Adolescent Psychiatry "as many as half of all children are bullied at some time during their school years, and at least 10% are bullied on a regular basis." Kids can be cruel. But a particular challenge for an undocumented immigrant student is that, when these types of experiences occur, it can feel as if there is no one to turn to. A person without papers doesn't want to make waves at school for fear that doing so might lead to scrutiny, and possible deportation. Likewise, complaining to one's parents can present a challenge. After all, these parents have sacrificed everything to provide a better life for you, they're also struggling to acclimate, and it's not like they can go down to the school and advocate for their children without potentially putting themselves in jeopardy.

Dulce told me that, while she was grateful to her parents for bringing her and her siblings out of poverty, she also felt as if they didn't understand that America is not the land of opportunity it purports to be. Not when a person lacks access to the resources required to advocate for themselves and be supported by society.

"I didn't feel comfortable going to school," Dulce recounted. "And I couldn't tell my parents, so I just had to pretend it wasn't affecting me in any way—but it was."

The transitional period of acclimating to a new life in a new school and a new society can be difficult even if a person isn't being actively excluded. Of her moves from Ecuador to Canada, back to Ecuador again, then to the United States, Sulafa told me "In hindsight, I can see that it was traumatic. I remember having a hard time adjusting. I'm honestly pretty sure I was in some kind of mild depression, but it was never diagnosed. I was a teenager, in the middle of shaping my personality, shaping my social circle, creating a support system outside of the house... Navigating all these changes was tough."

It's not surprising that many who relocate to another country suffer in the early stages of social adaptation. Change is difficult and it can be especially challenging for those who aren't choosing it for themselves.

Veronica Fitzgerald, who came to the United States from Ecuador as a teenager, recalled in her interview with AnnaMarie, "The transition for me particularly was the hardest. I've always been a social butterfly, and, when my mom shared with us that we were to make this move, I didn't want to go. I would've done anything to stay in Ecuador. I said, 'Please don't take me with you.' My mom was very nonchalant. She said 'Listen, if someone can keep you—maybe, your grandparents, or uncle—you can stay. You don't have to come.'"

"But," Veronica chuckled—now, she can laugh about what at the time was devastating, "because I was a handful, nobody wanted me. So I went kicking and screaming."

Veronica struggled to find her place in a new society. "The first year was really hard for me," she remembered. "Socially, it was hard to adapt, even though I had all these great people around me. I had a bit of a nervous breakdown during my first year."

She told AnnaMarie about the breakdown itself and how powerless she and her family felt throughout it. "One day, I stayed in the same classroom for three periods without moving. I didn't switch classes until the teacher noticed. Then, I was sent to the nurse's office. The nurse kept asking me all these questions. She thought I had taken something. They called my brother down to talk to me and try to figure out what was up."

Veronica hadn't taken drugs, as the nurse suspected, but she had taken diet pills.

"When I came here, in those initial months of adjusting, I didn't realize it, but I was apparently depressed. My depression manifested itself in eating. I put on a lot of weight in the first six months and I was unhappy with that." After watching a commercial about diet pills, Veronica went to the store and bought some, which she began taking unbeknownst to anyone else. "They were filled with caffeine or something," she said, "so I was going through whatever physical reaction the pills were causing in my system. I still don't know exactly what was occurring except that, one day, I just felt unmotivated. I didn't feel like doing anything in school. The nurse thought I was under the influence and sent me to a hospital—a psychiatric hospital—to get bloodwork and urine samples done. Because my English was not the best, they kept me there and took me away from my mom. They basically told her, 'As of this moment, we are taking custody of your daughter and you just have to listen to us.' My mom said, 'She probably just wants to go back to Ecuador, and, if that's the case, I can send her back if that's what's going to make her happy.'"

Despite her mother's protestations, the hospital refused to release her daughter. Veronica spent three weeks institutionalized against her will before she was released. She told AnnaMarie that, in 2018, when children were being separated from their parents at the border and kept in cages and there was widespread media coverage about how these families were being separated and denied access to one another and to proper care and support, she was reminded of her own experience of being taken away from her parents.

Not only did Veronica feel empathy for the children who'd been locked in cages as a compassionate human, a member of the Latinx community, a mother, and an immigrant, but she felt for them as someone who had been separated from their parents against their will. So many others watched these same scenes on the news or read articles about the people arrested at the border and felt... nothing. There are deep ideological and etymological reasons for that.

Obed told me that "The system and the language has dehumanized the immigrant. To depict someone as illegal and alien has dehumanized immigrants. It is a big problem. Ethically, when somebody says 'illegal,' it is already making the person criminal which is why, I will not say all, but for most average Americans, to see the children in cages at the border doesn't bother them because for them, they are illegal. Therefore, automatically, in their mind, they deserve it—which is sick, because it is dehumanizing."

Over and over, I heard stories of Latinx immigrants being dehumanized by the system while being supported by smaller social networks—artist groups, small social collectives, and thriving community organizations. Those networks are important, especially because, in the absence of them, individuals can feel alienated and alone.

Because Dulce didn't find a community until relatively recently, she suffered a lot. When she got pregnant and she and her partner had their son, a joyful experience for many young parents, she felt like she was living an emotional reenactment of her adolescent years. Dulce recalled "I was always afraid that I didn't know how I was going to be able to raise another human being. Raising another human being in society is a big responsibility. I want my son to be kind to others and, at the same time, I want him to be able to be a strong person. When the time came, and he was born, I held him for the first time and I didn't feel anything. Neither happiness nor sadness. I guess because I'd worried too much during the pregnancy, I never felt a bond between the baby and I. I never asked myself if I had any love for the baby growing inside of me. The first month, it was just a baby and I. We wouldn't go outside because of how people usually reacted. If I went outside and my son started crying, I would hear comments from other people about how I wasn't taking good care of him, or I was being negligent. People were judging me based on stigmas and stereotypes. It took me a while to realize that it's normal for a baby to cry."

Now, six years later, Dulce can see that she was suffering from postpartum depression. Back then, she didn't have a community around her to support her in her struggle, and she didn't have access to the sort of medical benefits that might have really helped her.

One of my interviewees, Ivonne, chose not to share her last name due to her undocumented status and desire for anonymity. Through her translator Leah Margareta Gazzo Reisman, a bilingual nonprofit professional and sociologist, she told me, tears in her eyes, about how it wasn't until she found a community of strong and supportive women that she felt at home in the States. Ivonne said it was having her daughter that enabled her to seek that circle of support. She wants her daughter to see the world as full of unlimited opportunities and to believe in her own capabilities. So, she has surrounded herself with other strong females and they all bolster one another.

One thing that happens when we involve ourselves in communities is that we expand our perspective through learning and listening.

"Two of the big influences in my life have been Dr. Martin Luther King, with all the concepts of the beloved community," Obed informed me, "and Dr. Paulo Freire, the Brazilian educator, who practiced what is called "biological education" which is education in which the teacher and the student talk and listen to each other and education becomes horizontal. Everybody has something to teach and everybody has something to learn."

The concepts of listening as a deliberate action and being heard as a path to demonstrating one's own value came up a lot. As Sulafa said, "If we can take the action to be a generous listener, to hear the narratives of those around us and become attuned to the struggles and the successes of others, we open ourselves up to opportunities for creativity and connection."

When we feel seen and heard and known and believe that we are both liberated by our various intersecting and overlapping communities and by a force for the liberation of others within these communities, the walls within us and between us begin to come down.

As AnnaMarie put it, "I see fear as a wall—an intangible wall."

Despite all the barriers she'd faced throughout her middle and high school years, despite not having any friends at school and being bullied, Dulce persisted. She studied diligently and graduated high school as the valedictorian of her 2013 class.

"I thought about dropping out of high school many times to get a job," she said, "but I wanted to obtain a diploma. I wanted the opportunities that would come with that."

On the day of her graduation, Dulce approached the podium. The gathered families, faculty, administration, and the classmates who had shunned her and treated her cruelly were ready and receptive. Dulce had been silent, and silenced, for far too long. This was her opportunity to emerge. The speech she gave was both a testament to her accomplishments and a demonstration of her value and her voice. "Coming out of the shadows was the title of my speech, and it was what I did," she told me. "I openly told my immigration status. I said that, just because I was undocumented didn't mean I wasn't capable. It might take me a little more, but I can achieve what others can. And I said that, because I didn't have documents, I wasn't able to go to college."

For the undocumented members of American society, college accessibility differs based on your state of residence. In some states, undocumented immigrants are refused admittance altogether. In others, they are forced to pay much higher out-of-state tuition, despite being in-state residents. There are states that support social mobility by offering immigrant students in-state tuition and financial aid but policies vary by location and institution.

In Dulce's case, the cost to attend college would have been triple the cost for other in-state residents. Never mind that she wanted to continue her studies, or that she had academically outperformed every single person in her graduating class, post-secondary educational opportunities weren't possible. Despite this disappointment, Dulce focused on what was possible and explored alternate vehicles for advancement.

"In 2013, which is the year I graduated, I received my ED, which is an employment authorization document," she informed me. "I was then allowed to legally work in the United States. That has opened up many opportunities in terms of jobs. I have done so many jobs. I have worked in restaurants, companies, supermarkets. My ED opened the opportunity to have fair treatment wherever I go and work."

We need to let go of the misplaced notion that the American nation can thrive on a stagnant employment and educational pool. We require immigrants to stimulate the economy, increase labor opportunities, and add to the influx of new ideas. There are tangible, documented, and statistically supported benefits to an influx of both documented and undocumented immigrants.

"The research consistently finds that the first generation, so people who are born outside the U.S. and arrive when they are young, have the lowest engagement of criminal activity," John MacDonald told me. "The second generation, so that means you're born in the U.S. but your parents are from overseas or another country, still has lower delinquency. It's really in the third generation where there's no difference. So, it's actually the opposite of what a lot of people think and the narratives that have become part of popular discourse that either immigrants themselves or their kids are going to join a gang or something. No. Those kids are at lower risk of joining a gang. It's really the grandkids who have the same likelihood of criminality as any other American. So, if you think about that, it no longer becomes an immigration story. It becomes a story about economic assimilation and upward mobility."

Sulafa wouldn't be in law school now, had she not been afforded opportunities for upward social mobility. She credits her undergraduate college (City University of New York) and her many personal and professional mentors for her ability to advance without stopping—or even slowing down.

"CUNY does a really good job at supporting students as they work towards social mobility and actually achieve their next steps," she told me. "You still pay tuition, but it's significantly less costly. I entered a community college not because I didn't pass my SATS or didn't get a good score, but my mom was just establishing our home and couldn't afford tuition. The point of continuing education is to advance so that you can earn a revenue that will support your needs and support your family. I was very capable at 17, when I graduated high school, but, had I not had access to a community college, I would have had to wait three or four years to work and make enough funds to enter college. CUNY offered a vehicle for my social mobility."

By and large, Americans who oppose immigration have not taken the time to familiarize themselves with the statistics. According to Unidos US, the average immigrant-owned business hires 11 employees and, taken as an aggregate, these businesses provide between 3.7 million and 5.2 million jobs, every year, undocumented immigrants pay an average of $11.64 billion in state and local taxes, and immigrants have contributed up to $300 billion to the Social Security Trust Fund. Immigrants enrich the American economy and, therefore, enabling educational opportunities for motivated and earnest individuals offers much more than a catalyst for their forward-momentum. It offers tremendous value to the social collective.

We would do well to recognize the contributions the Latinx immigrant community, and other communities, make to American society and to configure public policy in such a way that it enables their success.

As the system is configured, some Latinx immigrant students are being afforded the requisite vehicles for social mobility while others are not and still others have been able to avail themselves of and involve themselves with supportive social and community networks. But this selective social mobility isn't sufficient. We need to embrace those who come to this country seeking to contribute to the social collective through employment, entrepreneurship, and education, which we can only do if we dismantle the language of "illegal" and "alien."

I admire anyone who has the gumption and the guts to leave what is known for what is unfamiliar, to completely uproot themselves and/or their families and demonstrate their capacity for growth by traveling thousands of miles and establishing a new life. Being an immigrant, documented or not, requires resilience, innovation, and adaptability. Sulafa told me, "it has always been part of my identity to be adaptable." It would have to be. Immigrants find the internal and external resources to create something out of nothing, often operating against all odds, and they find different ways of doing this.

Ivonne involved herself in a community of women. Sulafa discovered the value of mentorship and began giving back to others. Dulce worked and studied and eventually found an outlet in art. There are many ways to become integrally interwoven into the fabric of society—as many ways as there are individuals. This nation thrives on immigrant labor, innovation, cooperation, and social participation so it is both hypocritical and inhumane that we write so many immigrants out of the script of existence.

"We do not exist for the system," Obed told me. "An example of this occurred during COVID-19. You may remember that there was a stimulus package given to everyone—$1,200 per adult, more for those with kids. Immigrant families were not subject to receive that stimulus package, even in the midst of a pandemic. Why? Because we do not exist for the system."

In the case of the 250 families that are part of the active and vibrant community that is CCATE, these overlooked and underserved individuals came together to provide resources for all and to ensure that no one went hungry. But they shouldn't have had to. Latinx families shouldn't be treated like outsiders and outcasts.

As Veronica Fitzgerald said, "We have to truly look at what's happening in front of us and in the world around us and ask ourselves, over and over again, is this fair? Is this right? The perception is: Who are you to come to my country, and why do I have to pay for you to be here? What do you do for us? But, if you really look around, who are your service people? Who are the people that don't mind doing the jobs that most Americans do not want to do? We are the people doing those jobs—Latin American immigrants. There are desperate humans who are dying of hunger and they come here and show their grit and refuse to allow their circumstances to overshadow their potential. I count myself as one of those people, because I am an immigrant. Of course, I'm an American citizen now and I've lived here for over 30 years, but I was and will always be one of them."

The Latin American immigrant population offers an example of what becomes achievable when people work hard on behalf of themselves, their families, and their communities and, also, can be a counterbalance to the romantic but ultimately fragmenting idea of individualism at all costs.

To find a more expansive sense of equity within American society, it would behoove us to look to the Latin American immigrant population as a powerful example of what becomes achievable when people tap into the deeper parts of themselves and work hard for the advancement of themselves and those around them and give back to the community.

Adeija Jones, an Afro indigenous vegan activist with an ancestral lineage from Africa and Guatemala told me that her activism springs from an awareness of the interconnectedness of humanity and the importance of honoring our cultural predecessors. She said, "I try to understand that the world isn't here for me. I'm here for the world."

Dulce told me that the reason she agreed to be interviewed was because she hoped my project might help to "change the idea that other people might have about us—about immigrants and undocumented people—and to help others see that we can be important members of society." I hope that her story has done that and that, instead of erecting physical and/or emotional walls that limit our capacity to learn from and collaborate with one another, we can instead become attuned to the positive potential that exists within all of the individuals that comprise the collective.

If you have the companion *Demystifying Diversity Workbook*, please turn to the exercises for Chapter 11 and start them. Return to Chapter 12 in this book when you have completed them.

12   **Running Together**

> "You can't survive in this kind of climate without mutual understanding. That's interracial relationship 101. We both try to think from the other person's perspective. That definitely strengthens the relationship."
>
> Emmanuel Aouad, Business Process Optimization
> Program Manager, musician and videographer

Emmanuel and Ashlee Aouad showed up for their Zoom interview wearing matching shirts, the same bright red shade you'd associate with Valentine's Day hearts. They'd gotten dressed separately and hadn't coordinated what they would wear, which made the unexpected synchronicity all the sweeter. Our interview fell on the six-year anniversary of the day Emmanuel sent Ashlee an opening message on Match.com.

Would you rather me start with a joke or a corny pickup line? the subject line read.

She didn't directly answer what they now both agree was a cheesy opener, but they began a back-a-forth correspondence that led to a first date. The date lasted from 5:00 in the evening until two a.m. the following morning.

"We just kept extending it." Ashlee remembered.

Emmanuel reached out to take her hand. "Yeah. I expected it to be a good date, but it was unprecedented."

"I knew from the moment I met him that he was my person," Ashlee exalted. "I was like 'Oh. There you are...'"

Emmanuel and Ashlee share passions, hobbies and interests. They're *Harry Potter* fans, they love sampling new cuisines, and they care a lot about fitness. Something they often do together is run, although to say they do it "together" is a bit misleading. Emmanuel always runs in front of Ashlee. She insists on it. An impassioned May 27, 2020 Facebook post explains why:

Important personal update about my husband and me... So I pretty much only ever post stuff about my fitness business but I wanted to share a personal update with you all (fair warning, this post might be disturbing). I really appreciate your support of my husband and I during this difficult time.

I'll start with the good news—my husband and I have been having a lot of fun getting out for runs together lately!

The bad news and the update is—running is one of the most anxiety producing things we do together.

My husband usually runs in front of me for two reasons—the first reason is because he is faster than me and the second reason I will share momentarily.

Because he runs in front of me I get to watch him the whole time I'm running—which means I see every time a car drives past him. Sometimes the car drives really slowly and I spend a few seconds agonizing about why they are driving slower and wondering if they're about to ask him if he "lives around here" and attack him if they aren't happy with his answer. I envision a gun barrel poking out the window of the car and shooting my beautiful, perfect, kind husband in the face. Every. Time.

The second reason my husband always runs in front of me is I don't want someone to think he is chasing me if he runs behind me. White women have a horrible pattern of falsely accusing [B]lack men of atrocities—and that narrative is in your head whether you know it or not. So if someone called 911 out of fear for my fragile [W]hite life and told them a [B]lack man was chasing a [W]hite woman down the street—they wouldn't think twice about dispatching officers immediately. And I'm terrified of what would happen then.

We have a rule in our house that if we ever have to call the police to our home that I will be the one to answer the door—because I'm afraid they'll think my husband is the reason they were called and they'll kill him first and ask questions later.

If you're reading this, you probably know my husband. Funny, thoughtful, nerdy, outgoing, caring, sweet Emmanuel. You know him.

I want you to picture it was him being pinned to the ground under an officer's knee—slowly suffocating and then eventually passing away. I want you to picture it was him bird watching in the park and a [W]hite woman PURPOSELY told the police an AFRICAN AMERICAN MAN WAS THREATENING HER LIFE. SHE DID THAT SHIT ON PURPOSE. SHE KNEW EXACTLY WHAT COULD HAPPEN IF THE POLICE HEARD SOMETHING LIKE THAT.

We don't have children yet but I'm terrified of what might happen to them. I think of the little 15-year-old [B]lack girl at a pool party in a town less than ten miles from us, who was thrown to the ground in her bathing suit by a police officer who then proceeded to slam her head in to the grass repeatedly, then kneeled on top of her back.

How are we supposed to bring children in to this world? What rules will I have to teach them that I didn't grow up with myself? "Sweetie, I'm sorry I know it's cold in the grocery store but you can't wear your hoody inside—people might think you're trying to steal something." "Darling, never ever ever speed but also don't drive *too* slowly—you don't want to give a police officer an excuse to pull you over because when you reach for your ID, they might think you're pulling a gun and shoot you on sight. And no one will care because you were born with [B]lack skin, just like Daddy."

Black Lives Matter. If you disagree with that statement, unfriend me. On here and in real life. If you don't know what Black Lives Matter really means—ASK!

For those of you (specifically [W]hite people) who made it this far, this is where I need your support. If you are a [W]hite person, post SOMETHING about your feelings about recent events (which of course aren't just recent—but focusing on the ones that are in the news right now is a good place to start). We have a responsibility to use our privilege to amplify the [B]lack voices that are constantly dismissed. We have to try. It feels hopeless, but we have to try.

Write something. It doesn't have to be perfect. Just try. Make an effort. You never know if there is someone in your sphere of influence who subconsciously thinks some really dark things—and maybe, just maybe, you can help get inside their heads and change their thinking—before it's too late for yet another person of color.

As she says in her post, Ashlee is White. Emmanuel is Black. She worries a lot about his safety. "I'll worry when he goes to the grocery store, if he's taking too long. This is a big, strong, muscular man. This guy does Ninja Warrior workouts, and it says a lot that I worry about him going to the grocery store. One time, he had to go out kind of late at night to get me some medicine and I was scared. I was worried the whole time. I was like, *What are they going to think about him going to the grocery store? It's about to close. What was he wearing? Was he wearing something that someone might see and get suspicious?* Thoughts like that will constantly pop into my head and I wouldn't have those worries if I was with a White partner."

Emmanuel doesn't generally stress about that stuff although he acknowledged that "When it comes to racism, all it takes is one person. One person can be the difference between you living and you dying." He told me that he puts his focus elsewhere. "The biggest F-you I can give somebody, especially somebody who believes that I shouldn't live my life a certain way, or I'm lesser than them, is to live an amazing life."

For Emmanuel and Ashlee, part of living an amazing life has involved a willingness to learn and grow from cultures other than those they were born into.

"Just being open to the idea of marrying someone outside of my immediate circle has enriched my life so much in the last six years," Emmanuel said.

"If I hadn't been raised to only look for a partner who was going to care for me, and be nice to me, and be a good support system, if I had ever had any kind of boxes put around partners that I could look for, I could have potentially never met you and I can't even imagine," Ashlee told him. "I can't imagine what my life would be like without you. I love you so much."

"I love you, too," he replied.

They told me that their families had always supported and encouraged their relationship. In fact, Emmanuel told me about a conversation he had with Ashlee's family approximately four weeks prior to our interview. "I'd never told them before, but I was like, 'I want to let you know how much I appreciate that, since the first moment we met, you've always interacted with me on a person level." He explained that, in the past, he'd had friends and dated girls "whose families have interacted with me based on how they think I want to be interacted with, based on what they think black people enjoy.'"

He and Ashlee moved closer together on their couch. "You can hit it off with somebody," he continued, "but you also need to be able to blend in with their family for it to be a great relationship."

Although Ashlee and Emanuel sometimes feel exhausted by the racism and discrimination that exists in the world outside their immediate circle, they have connected so much with each other and with one another's families that they don't want anything about their unit to change. Instead, they want society to be different.

Throughout my interviews with interracial couples, I noticed that all of their relationships shared the same trait: The couple had either consciously or unconsciously made the decision that they wouldn't allow society to dictate their decisions. Despite possible societal pressures, each couple told me that their love was stronger because they didn't color inside society's arbitrary racial, cultural and ethnic lines.

Chris Jones, AnnaMarie's husband, told me "Being married to a Biracial woman has really opened my eyes to White male privilege and has allowed me to explore firsthand the experiences, challenges, and perceptions of others."

He said he sees AnnaMarie's Biraciality as an asset and he admires her for the empathy she's developed and the advocacy she's adopted because of her invisible diversity. AnnaMarie is White-passing yet having a Black dad who grew up in the segregated South taught her the importance of equity and inclusion and, as a White-passing woman, she has used her access to various spaces as a platform to educate others about the impact of prejudice and encourage them to examine their privilege.

"Her dad would be so proud of what she's doing," Chris said.

AnnaMarie got a little teary. "It wasn't safe for him to stand up. He had to keep his head down and he really suffered. It was exhausting to fight and exhausting not to."

Elizabeth Hasegawa Agresta and Thomas Agresta haven't felt as if they've had to struggle against society as much as some other interracial couples. They attribute this to living on the East Coast and to their ability to unplug.

"We can turn off the news and just focus on our little unit here. No matter how insane it gets, it's continued to be pretty healthy at our house. We have a solid unit to come back to," Elizabeth told me. Elizabeth is Asian. Thomas is White. They've been together since 1990. I met them because the eldest of their three kids, Yoshiko, went to school with my sister. The Agrestas are a very connected, loving family. When Yoshiko, Jimmy, and Paul were growing up, the five of them had dinner together at home almost every night and did things as a unit on the weekends.

The pair met at Threads and Treads, a well-known running store on Greenwich Avenue in Greenwich, Connecticut, the major shopping street in the center of town. Elizabeth had recently moved to Greenwich from Canada to pursue a career in nursing. She and Thomas are both avid runners and, being relatively new to the area and seeking opportunities to surround herself with likeminded people, Elizabeth had registered for the Greenwich Avenue one-miler.

As she recalls it, "I went into the store where they were selling the registrations and I asked them what the directions were. I got laughed at."

Thomas shook his head, smiling, still bemused even after the passage of thirty years, "It's one mile straight down Greenwich Avenue."

Elizabeth continued. "Thomas was in the store with a group of other guys and we got to talking."

"We met later that week and went for a five-mile run," Thomas added, "then showered and went to dinner at–"

Elizabeth interrupted. "Showered at our individual places."

We all smiled at the clarification.

"Consider that on the record." I laughed. "Wouldn't want people thinking otherwise."

The couple told me that their different racial, ethnic and geographic backgrounds felt inconsequential.

"I looked at our commonalities more than anything," Elizabeth said. "We both liked to run. He was interested in doing things like ceramics and pottery, he came from a family with a lot of kids, gets along with his parents... We shared so much. I didn't look any deeper than that."

"Yeah," Thomas agreed. "I feel like, with our lives and our upbringings, we've lived the same story, just in different places."

Although Elizabeth told me that there were certain places where she might not want to show up with her husband, places where "I'd want to take the temperature of the room before going in," she and Thomas have always felt comfortable navigating life as an interracial couple, but that doesn't mean they haven't felt individually stereotyped.

"I think, even as our country gets older and older and generations go past, we still make assumptions about people based on the way that they look. I don't think anyone's immune to that. I mean, we do it, people do it to us, and they have no idea where you're coming from unless they talk to you and ask you what your background is, what your interests are, what kind of food you eat," Elizabeth said. She often encounters people who assume things about her because of her Asian identity.

"I've had a doctor talk to me on the phone and make a racial slur against Asians. He didn't realize who he was talking to. I was a little in shock over that."

In some ways, it can be easier to deal with other people's prejudice when the person misjudging you is a stranger, but, in other ways, it's gratifying to create connections that dispel societal stigmas. In the case of William and Marissa Gwynn, Marissa's family's lack of exposure to diversity made them initially reticent to approve of Marissa (who is White) dating a Black man. But the happily married couple told me that whatever early reservations were there are long gone. This isn't always the case.

For Armee and Michelle, who goes by the nickname Chelle, familial and societal stigmas may never completely go away. The wives are both first-generation Americans. Armee's parents are from the Philippines and Chelle's are from the Dominican Republic. They grew up with a lot of overlapping values and ethics.

"How we were brought up and raised is kind of similar," Chelle told me. "We grew up with a lot of love, but it was tough love."

Armee nodded. "My parents definitely taught me to be independent. They encouraged me to figure things out for myself. They wanted to prepare me for the world—because we were not going to get any handouts."

"It kind of trickles down to our relationship," Chelle explained. "We depend on each other, but we also don't take each other for granted. Finding individuality, being independent, but also coming together as a whole, is something we really value."

Chelle and Armee want to enact the values they were taught in terms of displaying grit and determination. However, there are other areas in their lives that they vehemently reject the messages their parents gave them.

"I can remember my parents saying 'You can have Black friends, but don't marry one.'" Armee gave Chelle a peck on the cheek.

Chelle laughed. "Don't marry one. Right."

"In your face," Armee replied. "I married one."

Armee and Chelle told me that, in their relationship, stigmas about sexuality overshadowed those they experienced because of race. They are both women and they both come from cultures that have tended to have fixed ideas about gender and sexuality.

"I think both race and sexuality are intertwined in some way with how other people have reacted to our relationship," Armee explained. "The race part is underneath. It's not so obvious—micro aggressions, rather than blatant racism."

"Good thing you mentioned that," Chelle said. "I feel like to be gay within my communities, Black and Hispanic, is a no. People have been opening up more, but back when we met, it was something you wouldn't talk about."

They told me that being members of the LGBTQIA+ community in families that subscribed to heteronormative ideals has enabled them to let go of trying to live up to other people's expectations and given them the freedom to be themselves.

I wondered, out loud, if they thought that, if they'd fallen in love with and married men, their families would have felt differently about their interracial relationship.

Armee was the first to answer. "In some ways, it would have been easier, but then it also would have been harder because, if either of us really subscribed to the cultural values we grew up with—that macho bullshit—that wouldn't have worked for my temperament. I want my input to be valued and respected. I want to compromise and make things work as partners. At the same time, in some ways, it would be easier because then my family could be like, 'Oh, Armee married a man.'"

"So," I reflected, "it would have been externally easier but internally harder."

They nodded simultaneously—on the same page as each other about not being on the same page as others.

"I think our relationship has allowed us to beat the stereotypes and be like, okay, this is what you think of us," Chelle said. "Well, no, we're going to show our love the way we see it. And it actually helped us become stronger."

Although Armee and Chelle don't have children yet, they spoke about the ways in which they want to raise their future offspring to see their interracial, multiracial, and cross-cultural household as a gorgeous kaleidoscope—so many variations and variables, beautiful and captivating. They hope that their children will have positive perceptions of race and culture and are seeking to learn in advance how best to handle their racial education.

For Thomas and Elizabeth, whose kids are grown now, they have the benefit of hindsight and can see what it was like for their kids to be raised by parents of different races. Elizabeth told me that their son, Paul, sometimes gets made fun of because "His friends have told him that I'm super Asian. They make fun of him about me, and I think that makes him want to deny the Asian part of himself."

The Agrestas' daughter, Yoshiko, experienced race-based othering as well.

When she was in the first grade, a Japanese exchange student arrived in her class and the teacher assumed that, based on Yoshiko's name and appearance, she spoke the language. She instructed Yoshiko to translate.

"Yoshiko laughed in the teacher's face," Thomas recalled. "When she finally stopped, she looked straight at the teacher and said, 'I don't know Japanese.'"

Elizabeth smiled. "That taught her teacher a lesson."

Malynda Hale and John Volk had their first child a few months ago. As new parents, they are finding their way—not that they haven't been discussing for a long time how they'd raise a child.

"Malynda is big on hypotheticals," John told me. "When you're with her, there's always the possibility of a pop-quiz."

The famous singer, a striking Black woman with a radiant spirit and overflowing energy and her sarcastic and self-deprecating White lawyer husband have different personalities and upbringings. They hope their daughter inherits elements of both of them. They are already teaching her to value the rich spectrum of human diversity.

"I never want to take away from our daughter the part of her that is her father," Malynda said, "but I want to make sure that she knows the part of her that's me—no matter what society is telling her is of value and of worth. She's beautiful. It's important to expose children to all sorts of people. It's like when Disney finally had a Black princess and you think about all of those little Black girls that would go to Disneyland dressed as Belle, dressed as Cinderella, because that's all they knew. And then they're like, 'oh my God, I have a Black princess now.' It's a huge deal to have something that represents you and that you can relate to. We have a huge book collection for her. She's three and a half months old we're already making her take the SATs, showing her all these books."

Malynda grew up in California and John grew up in Kansas. She's an extroverted singer, songwriter, and activist. He's a somewhat introverted attorney. They are both unapologetically themselves and they attribute their relationship longevity at least in part to their authenticity.

"I was exactly who I was, right from the get go," John said.

Their early relationship was a whirlwind long-distance romance that culminated in marriage. There were moments when outside prejudices put a damper on their inner bliss. On one occasion, they were walking down the street in downtown Chicago when a Black taxi driver pulled up in front of them, rolled down his window, and yelled at Malynda "You better change your tune, sister."

He drove off, leaving John confused. It took several seconds to figure out that the man had been calling Malynda a traitor to her race for dating a White man.

"So much of being White is not realizing that these things are happening to people of color all the time," John said. "You have to be personally affected by something unless you're really extraordinarily perceptive."

John told me that being with Malynda has emboldened him to engage in difficult conversations head-on and not to let racism go unchecked, although he's not always as perceptive given that he didn't experience any racial moments until meeting, and then marrying Malynda.

"It sounds like those were new experiences for you, John," I reflected. "Were those new experiences for you, Malynda?"

"Not at all," she replied. Then, she repeated it. "Not at all. I dated a bunch of races before I met John, and the vitriol that I've met with dating White men from Black men is very abrupt. But then the racism that I've experienced from White families or White friends has always been very subtle."

I asked her how she'd felt about the moment on the street with John and all the similar moments that have occurred throughout her interracial relationships.

"It's hard to navigate," she said, "because you're happy and then here's this random stranger that's trying to encroach upon your happiness for no reason. It's like, okay, well, how are you going to navigate that together?"

Malynda and John have found ways to not only navigate but to celebrate their love. "We celebrate Loving Day every year when

Richard and Mildred Loving were able to get married," Malynda told me.

In 1958, Richard and Mildred Loving had been married for five weeks when police burst into their home in the middle of the night and arrested them for violating Virginia's Racial Integrity Act. According to Virginia state law, it was a crime for Richard, of Irish and English descent, and Mildred, African American and Native American, to have gotten married. The Lovings were tried and found guilty of the "crime" of interracial marriage and given the choice to either go to prison or to leave Virginia for 25 years. The Lovings left. But they didn't give up. Missing their lives and their families in Virginia, they fought the Virginia judge's decision. It took nine years but, finally, in a unanimous Supreme Court decision handed down for Loving v. Virginia on June 12, 1967, laws banning interracial marriage were deemed unconstitutional.

"I do a long social media post about it," Malynda said. "A lot of people don't even know that it's a thing. I talk about our relationship and that we're grateful we're able to be together. People are very surprised that that case was only 53 years ago, 19 years before we were born. I like to share that information. I had somebody write to me, *What? Interracial relationships were illegal?* How can someone not know that? I like to educate on that day every year."

"So," I clarified, "it's more of a public-facing celebration than a private one?"

"Exactly." She laughed. "We celebrate Loving Day every day."

The interracial couples I interviewed have expanded their perspectives and enriched their lives by deliberately engaging with diversity. They might not always feel as if they're able to run side by side. Other things can get in the way—societal stigmas, worry, the occasional misunderstanding—but they are heading in the same direction, motivating and inspiring one another to go faster and farther, and to journey together on the winding road of love.

If you have the companion *Demystifying Diversity Workbook*, please turn to the exercises for Chapter 12 and start them. Return to Chapter 13 in this book when you have completed them.

13 Putting the Glass Back Together

"Because love is an act of courage, not of fear, love is a commitment to others. No matter where the oppressed are found, the act of love is commitment to their cause—the cause of liberation."

Paulo Freire, educator, philosopher and advocate

In 2019, months after I accompanied Holocaust survivor Bill Schwabe and his friend to the National Liberty Museum for a guided tour, I joined them both at their assisted living facility for an early-bird dinner. I arrived to find them waiting for me in the lobby.

"Daralyse!" Bill exclaimed. "How are you?"

"I'm great," I answered. "How are you?"

His eyes sparkled. "You know, the world is in pain, but I'm happy to be alive and happy to be in good company."

I handed him the copy of his unpublished memoir that he'd loaned me. He put it into the basket of his red motorized scooter. Bill joked that he got the red scooter to let everyone know that he was a fast and flashy driver—never mind that the scooter's speed didn't ever climb above three miles an hour. He led the way—his bright red motorized scooter inching forward at a snail's pace, his friend and I following, her using her walker and me matching her stride. We were an unlikely trio as we made our way to the facility's formal dining room and sat down. In this retirement community, food was served early and overcooked, but we weren't there because we cared about the culinary quality. We were there for connection and conversation.

Having read Bill's memoir, I had so many questions about his involvement in civil rights and inclusion. Bill had worked in public service and hospital administration for decades. He had been actively involved in petitioning for equal wages for Black medical workers and equal treatment for Black patients in the 1960s and 70s. He advocated against sexual harassment in the workplace.

"I think," he told us between bites of rubbery roast beef, "every human being deserves to feel valued and loved." We talked about the egregious treatment of immigrants at the border, the importance of equity initiatives and how true patriotism requires questioning the status quo. Bill was outspoken about the issues, even using more than a few expletives when referring to President Trump. We talked, too, about his granddaughters, his son, Andy, and his late wife and forever love, Norma.

Bill didn't seem to be irrevocably scarred by any of the elements of his past. He was happy to have been a part of the world even if now he felt shut out from the stream of life. He entertained us with stories about his experiences in the armed forces.

"Do you know that, when I was overseas in Germany, serving in the war, I actually ran into my old elementary school teacher—the one who'd beaten me and called me names for being Jewish? He was an officer in the SS and he'd been brought in for questioning." He took a bite of dinner roll. "He looked so small and scared then. Bullies are really all afraid at the core."

I wanted to know about his love story with his wife, whom he described as "my much, much better half." Our fellow dinner companion had met Norma before she passed and she told me stories about the two of them playing tricks on one another and kissing in the halls while Bill contributed tiny details, such as his memories of the way his wife's hair sometimes fell into her eyes and how she'd brush it back with a sigh and a smile.

Two hours flew by. When it was time to leave, Bill escorted me to the door and we gave each other an awkward hug goodbye—awkward because of the physical barriers posed by his scooter. It was impossible to be emotionally awkward with Bill. He had a way of putting everyone lucky enough to meet him at ease.

"See you soon, Daralyse," he said.

"Yes," I replied. "See you soon."

We never saw each other again. The pandemic hit in March and we maintained our connection with phone calls every four to six weeks during which we shared stories—me about the present, him about the past. As COVID-19 death tolls spiked, he worried about the disparity in death rates within communities of color.

I worried about him.

"Don't fret, Daralyse." His tone was light and unaffected. "When all this is over, we'll have another dinner and catch up properly."

In late June, Bill called to discuss his unpublished memoir. "Do you think there's any value to my story?" he asked. "Should I try to get it published?"

I told him, sincerely, that I'd loved so much about the story but that it ended in 1991 and I wanted him to add more. He had so many more rich life experiences to share. His story hadn't stopped in the nineties.

"Talk to Andy," I advised. "See if your son has any ideas about how to update it to span the past and the present. Then, call me next week."

"I'll call you Monday," he promised.

Monday came and went, and then Tuesday. Bill had never not called as arranged. I tried him. He didn't answer and didn't call back. I called again. Another message went unreturned. Concerned, I phoned his aide, Angela. In an anxious tone, she informed me that Bill was sick with a urinary tract infection (UTI).

"We're not sure what's going to happen. I pray he'll be okay."

Despite my concerns about Bill contracting COVID-19, I wasn't especially nervous about a UTI. Even at 96, Bill had always seemed somewhat invincible. He'd lived through war, the Holocaust and so many other trials and tribulations. I was looking forward to our next meal and hearing more of his stories about his long and love-filled life.

Then, on July 10th, 2020, a few months before the publication of this book, I received a phone call from Bill Schwabe's son, Andy. He told me that his father had died three days earlier, on July 7th. Andy and I had spoken before. A person couldn't be in Bill's life without getting to know his circle of supporters.

"Thank you so much for letting me know," I told him. "I loved your Dad."

"Yeah," he agreed. "It was impossible not to love him."

Even though Andy's loss had been shattering, and his grief was only three-days old, we spent half an hour sharing memories about his dad and laughing about the unapologetic way Bill had lived.

"He was a real character, wasn't he?"

Before getting off the phone, Andy said, "You know, Daralyse, I want to thank you. Our society tends to devalue our elderly, but you didn't. You treated my dad like a human being. You saw his worth and that was really important. My dad appreciated that a lot. You enriched the end of his life by being in it."

I told Andy the truth—that his father had enriched my life in ways too numerous to convey. I was the lucky one, and I would miss him. Andy and I swore to stay in touch, and we have. He came to Philly to settle his dad's estate and we met for coffee. Connecting us is the adhesive of our affection for a man who cared about others and, in doing so, compelled others to care about him.

In speaking with more than 100 different individuals about their lives and losses, their traumas and their triumphs, I've learned that most of us want the same things. We want our basic needs for food, safety and shelter to be met, and, after that, we want to feel as if, at the end of our lives, we left the world better than when we found it. We want to believe that we were loved as ourselves and loved others in ways that made a tangible difference in their lives. None of us are perfect people, and none of us have lived perfect lives, but we want to be good and to do good in the world. And, even if we've made mistakes, which every one of us has, we want to be able to lock eyes with other people and know that they see our hearts and believe the best about us.

So many of the people I came to know and love since embarking on the Demystifying Diversity initiative are people I would never have crossed paths with otherwise. By connecting over our shared humanity, I have forged lasting friendships and learned a lot about the importance of empathy. Some of the people who have enriched my life the most are people with whom I don't share much on the surface. Yet, we have connected deeply. They've taught me so much and I consider our relationships to be sacred. I could never have figured out the lessons they've taught me without them entrusting me with their stories.

One of the people I interviewed for this project, Russell Murray, has become a good friend from behind bars. We met long before he gave me his on-the-record interview. About five years ago, I participated in a community service project where I was assigned the name of an inmate and tasked with sending them a book and a letter. I drew Russell's name, never suspecting that one letter would turn into a five-year-long correspondence.

I wrote to him, he wrote to me, I wrote again... We developed a pattern of regular communication. It wasn't long into our fledgling friendship that he called me out.

Why do you always ask me about me and not tell me more about you? he asked.

I told him the truth I feel bad that I'm on the outside, living a full life, and you're locked away. I guess I don't want to rub it in.

You kidding? he replied. I have a full life here. I'm not waiting until I get out to live. I've found friends and meaning right where I am.

Russell taught me a lot. Even in prison, he found ways to give back—saving the income he raised from his employment to buy meals for his contemporaries, connecting with his kids, and taking an active interest in the spiritual wellbeing of a stranger. I've lost count of how many times Russell has told me he's praying for me. Our relationship has evolved past me thinking I'm the one offering support. Instead, we're there for each other.

I tell him about my writing life, my latest dating disasters, and my unrealized dreams for the future. He encourages me to keep reaching. *One day,* he promises, *God's gonna give you everything you ask for. Never lose sight of all that's possible.*

Every few months for five years, Russell and I have written to one another, first with snail-mail letters and now through the prison email system. When I embarked on the *Demystifying Diversity Podcast* project, I asked if he would speak to me on the record, on the phone. *Anything you need*, he replied. *I'm happy to help.*

After the project wrapped, Russell and I arranged a video visit during which we saw each other for the first time. We laughed together and caught up—once pen-pals, now friends. I went into our relationship thinking I had something to offer to an inmate and pretty quickly realized he was the one giving to me.

From speaking with people from all demographics and with a wide range of experiences, I've learned that the world would be better and safer if we would all embrace ourselves and each other, practice unconditional, inclusive love, stand up for one another, amplify the voices and the viewpoints of those who see the world differently than we do, and embrace the influx of newness that comes with opening our minds and hearts to the rich tapestry of human diversity.

I didn't set out to write this book to provide any answers, but rather to improve the quality of my questions and to inspire others to do the same. I wanted to make myself and others active in recognizing our awareness or lack thereof, pursuing understanding through questions and active listening, and engaging in diversity and inclusivity in tangible ways. Some of the things I continue to think about and trust that you will too are:

What opportunities become open to us if we embrace spectrum understandings of race? How can we be upstanders? How can we learn from and embrace various faith traditions? What are we doing to amplify marginalized voices? Where are we participating in oppression? How can we be forces for liberation? How can we expand beyond our preconceptions? What role can we play in our communities? What opens up when we become present to the redemptive power of love? Are we being generous listeners?

I believe that every one of us has things to teach and things to learn. It's only by embracing a horizontal understanding of humanity—in which we're all teachers and students, each able to contribute to our shared community, that we can grow together. Immersing myself in diversity and inclusion initiatives, I experience this type of learning on an almost daily basis.

I met Jon Quénard because both of us participated in emotional intelligence leadership trainings through Next Level Trainings, an incredible organization that has taught me how to connect with others through empathy, mutual support, and a willingness to tell and hear important truths. At first glance, I could tell that Jon was Biracial, like me. He is Asian and White and I am Black and White, but we didn't bond over that. Instead, we talked about our respective careers, our dating lives, our stumbling blocks, our successes, and how lit up we were by our respective missions. Jon is an essential early innovator at a tech start-up company and he's passionate about that and I've always been driven to transform the world through stories (whether my own stories, or the stories and experiences of others). We were on parallel paths of personal transformation and part of the same supportive community that Next Level Trainings creates for its student and graduates. We always had a very upfront friendship, but it wasn't until I started interviewing people that I decided to ask Jon about his experiences with race and culture. He told me about growing up in Switzerland and moving to the United States as a teenager and feeling like he was always a question mark, but, to quote him, "In a really positive way."

Towards the end of the question/answer period, the conversation meandered into a mutual discussion about mixed-race identity. Jon asked me how I felt about being Biracial. I thought for a moment, then replied "This probably won't make it onto the podcast" (and it didn't), "but I've felt, throughout my life, that there's a certain privilege that I hold as a multi-ethnic, Biracial person. I know that not all Biracial people experience it but, for me, I've always felt that I have access to a lot of spaces and that people are more open to me because I'm Biracial or even ethnically ambiguous."

"That really resonates for me, too," Jon said. "I feel that with race and I also feel it as someone who speaks multiple languages. I'm not just one thing or another. I'm both. It's like having two pairs of glasses. I can put on each set of glasses and see the world that way. I'll put my White pair of glasses and see the world that way, or my Asian glasses and see the world that way. I understand parts of each narrative, which makes reconciliation a bit easier. Is that how it is for you?"

"Sort of," I replied. "I've always believed that there's a distinct role that I can play because of my racial identity. I can't speak to the experience of being Asian and White, but as a Black/White person, especially in a country with a history of slavery and so many contentious race-relations and oppressions, where Blackness and Whiteness have been set up as binaries, just by virtue of my very identity, I push against that. I exist because, at least for as long as it took to conceive me, there was love and connection between a Black man and a White woman."

Jon and I laughed.

"Seriously," I continued, "a lot of people who are Biracial self-identify with only their minority race or try to pass as part of the White majority, but I identify as both. I want people to see me and see my example and know that it's possible for Whiteness and Blackness to exist simultaneously, in the same space, without any sort of conflict or challenge. I love my Blackness and I love my Whiteness and I think that pushes against a lot of what we are taught to believe about race."

I waited for Jon's reaction. I'm always open about my feelings about my ethnic identity but every mixed-race person's sense of their racial and ethnic identities has been shaped by their experiences, so I realize that my way of seeing Biracial identity isn't everybody's and I'm okay with that, although some people aren't okay with mine.

(You may recall the facilitator telling me, as a child, that the world would see me as Black to the exclusion of all else and that I should see myself that way too. That's not the only time someone's said that to me, but it is the earliest I remember having the conversation.)

Jon was excited by my perspective and adopted an aspect of it for himself. "The way you explained that... You're Black and White, and you love both, that's new to me. I've been identifying as I'm not fully Asian, and I'm not fully White, and I like the idea that I can be both and I can learn about and love both of them."

I was excited to have inspired Jon to have discovered a third option, so now he has his Asian glasses, his White glasses, and his both glasses, three perspectives with which to see the world and participate within it. Then, he shared something with me that I've tried to integrate, an idea that I didn't have access to until he expressed it.

"As I move forward in this world," Jon said, "I try to look at life through this lens of seeing every human being I meet as just another version of myself. When I come from that lens, of course I'm going to treat every person I encounter with kindness and love. Even if someone is pissing me off, I try to take a deep breath and remind myself that this person might become the most important person in my life."

This conversation with Jon perfectly encapsulates the mutual learning that happens when we engage with one another around issues of racial literacy and cultural competency.

At the time Jon and I spoke, I hadn't yet interviewed Obed Arango, who opened my eyes to the work of Paulo Freire. Now that I know about the Brazilian educator and philosopher, I know that to love the world is to seek to liberate it and that liberation can only happen via the vehicle of interpersonal and community connection. In *Pedagogy of the Oppressed*, Freire wrote, "This, then, is the great humanistic and historyical task of the oppressed: to liberate themselves and their oppressors as well."

Most of us have been oppressed at various times throughout our life, or possibly never not been oppressed, depending on the systemic nature of our struggles. Many of us may have actively participated in oppression, of others and of ourselves.

I didn't know how much I had to give until I interrogated my beliefs and biases. The process of dismantling my own baseless assumptions and interpretations, hearing the stories of others, and being vulnerable enough to admit that I am not the center of anything but one of the many beautiful and capable humans inhabiting this earth has provided me with a newfound capacity to love others and myself. I trust that the same process is available to everyone.

I hope that in grappling with the concepts in this book and engaging with the exercises in the suggested workbook, you have filled in some of the cracks in your heart and mind with the gold that comes from engagement and empathy. Life is made richer because of new ideas and resources and concepts and cultures. I hope you will continue to step outside yourself, into curiosity and connection, and to continue forward together in this journey to demystify diversity.

References

Ahmed, S., & Matthes, J. (2016). Media representation of Muslims and Islam from 2000 to 2015: A meta-analysis. International *Communication Gazette, 79*(3), 219-244. doi:10.1177/1748048516656305

Banerji, S. (2006, August 31). Study: Darker-skinned Black Job Applicants Hit More Obstacles. Retrieved August 30, 2020, from https://diverseeducation.com/article/6306/

Barakat, S. (2015, February 10). Islamophobia killed my brother. Let's end the hate. Retrieved September 04, 2020, from https://www.ted.com/talks/suzanne_barakat_islamophobia_killed_my _brother_let_s_end_the_hate?language=en

Burnley, M. (2015, March 13). My Biracial Life: A Memoir. Retrieved August 30, 2020, from https://www.phillymag.com/news/2015/02/08/my-biracial-life/

Drysdale, J. (2020, June 16). Who Is Matt James: 5 Things to Know About the First Black 'Bachelor'. Retrieved August 30, 2020, from https://www.etonline.com/who-is-matt-james-5-things-to-know-about-the-first-black-bachelor-148008

Farrell, D., Wheat, C., & Mac, C. (2020). Small Business Owner Race, Liquidity, and Survival. Retrieved August 30, 2020, from https://institute.jpmorganchase.com/institute/research/small-business/report-small-business-owner-race-liquidity-survival

Freire, P. (2018). Pedagogy of the oppressed. New York: Bloomsbury Academic.

Harrold, R. (2019). *My Buddha is pink: Buddhism for the modern homosexual*. Nepean, ON: The Sumeru Press Inc.

Hartke, A. (2018). *Transforming: The Bible and the lives of transgender Christians*. Louisville, KY: Westminster John Knox Press.

History.com Editors. (2017, November 17). Loving V. Virginia. Retrieved August 31, 2020, from https://www.history.com/topics/civil-rights-movement/loving-v-virginia

Idelson, S., Alpert, R. T., & Elwell, E. S. L. (2001). *Lesbian rabbis: The first generation*. New Brunswick, NJ: Rutgers University Press.

Jakobsen, J. R., & Pellegrini, A. (2004*). Love the sin: Sexual regulation and the limits of religious tolerance*. Boston, Mass: Beacon Press.

Markle, M. (2015, July 15). Meghan Markle: I'm More Than An 'Other'. Retrieved August 30, 2020, from https://www.elle.com/uk/life-and-culture/news/a26855/more-than-an-other/

Pattanaik, D. (2002). *The man who was a woman and other queer tales from Hindu lore*. Binghamton, N.Y.: HPP.

Metzl, J. (2020). *Dying of whiteness: How the politics of racial resentment is killing America's heartland*. New York: Basic Books.

Rusek, M. (2017, September 26). Autism found me, and then I found my voice. Retrieved August 30, 2020, from https://whyy.org/articles/essay-autism-found-me-and-then-i-found-my-voice/

Sienna, N. (2019). *A rainbow thread: An anthology of queer Jewish texts from the first century to 1969.* Philadelphia : Print-O-Craft.

Sizar, H. (2015). The Depiction of Muslim Americans in Children's Literature: A Case Study on the Children's Imprint Salaam Reads (Unpublished master's thesis). New York University.

Smith, A. (2005). The "Monster" in All of Us: When Victims Become Perpetrators. Retrieved August 30, 2020, from https://scholarship.law.georgetown.edu/facpub/219

Stevenson, H. (2017, November). How to resolve racially stressful situations. Retrieved August 30, 2020, from https://www.ted.com/talks/howard_c_stevenson_how_to_resolve_racially_stressful_situations?language=en

Stevenson, J., Harp, B., & Gernsbacher, M. (2011, October). Infantilizing Autism. Retrieved August 30, 2020, from https://dsq-sds.org/article/view/1675/1596

Thelos, P. (2004). *God is not a homophobe: An unbiased look at homosexuality in the Bible*. Victoria, B.C: Trafford.

Vera, A. (2020, May 26). White woman who called police on a black man bird-watching in Central Park has been fired. Retrieved August 30, 2020, from https://www.cnn.com/2020/05/26/us/central-park-video-dog-video-african-american-trnd/index.html

Vines, M. (2015). *God and the gay Christian: The biblical case in support of same-sex relationships*. New York: Convergent Books.

Williams, M., & Agresta, E. (2018). *"I'm mixed!"* Ann Arbor: Loving Healing Press.

Williamson, M. (1996). *A return to love: Reflections on the principles of a Course in miracles*. London: Thorson Classics.

Acknowledgements

I have no illusions that this book is my creation. More than a hundred incredible humans generously agreed to take time out of their lives to talk with me about diversity, to lend their voices to the *Demystifying Diversity Podcast*, and to provide the information that I've assembled and relayed in these pages.

It would be impossible to convey the depth of my gratitude. The process of learning from those I interviewed has radically transformed how I see the world and my hope is that it will do the same for you. But whether or not I do an effective job of transmitting what was transmitted to me, it's important to acknowledge that, without the generosity of others, this book would not exist.

Although it was impossible to incorporate every single voice from those I interviewed for season one of the *Demystifying Diversity Podcast* in a few hundred pages, I want to thank every single person who sat with me for an interview. Whether or not they were quoted directly, it is their collective wisdom that shines through in these pages and because there is no way to order their contributions, I will simply list their names alphabetically.

Many thanks to: Aaron Flores, Addison Kozuch, Adeija Jones, Ahmet Selim Tekelioglu, Alisa Kraut, Aliya Khabir, Angela Gardner, Armee Grace Campos, Arthur Kiron, Ashlee Aouad, Asma Rehman, August Terrier, Avery Kozuch, Aviv Haroz, Ben, Bibi Lorenzetti, Bill Schwabe, Brian Pollack, Caitie Corradino, Carly Bruski, Catherine Bartch, Cheryska Scanes, Chris Jones, Christopher Flanagan, Cinder Kuss, Danaijah Wilson, Dani Adriana, Daniel Bryerman, Dave Kyu, David Clizbe, Deborah Baer Moses, Dennis Moritz, Diana Clarke, Dion Lewis, Don Wyatt, Dulce Ramirez, Ed Eisen, Edward Cobbs, Jr., Elizabeth Bryerman, Elizabeth Hasegawa Agresta, Emily Zargan, Emmanuel Kwame Aouad, Gabe Goldstein, Gwen Borowski, Hanh Bui, Hediya Sizar, Howard Stevenson, Isabel Ballester, Ivonne, Izaneé Bryant, Jaiden Jones, Jaseem Giles, Jennifer Kreatsoulas, JoAnn George, Joe Finkelstein, John MacDonald, John Volk, John Wang, Jonah Bierig, Jon Quénard, Jose Gonzales, Joseph Green, Josh Perelman, Juan Rosa, Juliana Cabrales, Keren Friedman-Peleg, Kye' Shaun Hodge, Larry

Rubin, Leah Margareta Gazzo Reisman, Leilani Nieves, Lev Miller, Lewis Gantman, Liliana Cruz, Liliana Rodriguez, Makiyla Hampton, Malcolm Burnley, Malynda Hale, Marissa Gwynn, Marius Gherovici, Marta Gherovici, Marta Rusek, Matthew Newell, Max Scholl, Melissa Tsui, Michelle (Chelle) Campos-Velez, Milind Gandhi, Mona Masood, Nadine Rosechild Sullivan, Nancy Schwartz, Natalie Borowsky, Nihad Awad, Nikky, Noah Berman, Obed Arango, Oliver de Luz, On-Cho Ng, Paul Reese, Paula Goldstein, Pawel Sawicki, Pia Eisenberg, Rebecca Lerman, Rob O'Neil, Ruby Schwartz, Russell Murray, Russita Buchanan, Salaah Muhammad, Salima Suswell, Sarah Gandhi, Sharif Street, Skyler Sholder, Stacey Cunitz, Steve Mallon, Steve Weitzman, Sulafa Grijalva, Tayler Monts, Teri Scott, Thomas Agresta, Timaree Schmit, Tulia Falleti, Vara Cooper, Veronica Fitzgerald, William Gwynn, Yadin Isaacs, and those who opted to remain anonymous—the gender nonconforming parent of a trans-identifying child and the aspiring police officer.

Thank you to all of those who worked behind the scenes to facilitate coordinating interviews and connecting me with their employers, family members and friends. There were so many whose efforts enabled the interviews to happen and I want to especially recognize Becky Friedman (Communications Coordinator at the Herbert D. Katz Center for Advanced Judaic Studies), Catherine Lee (Development and Communications Manager at the Asian Arts Initiative), David Manning (Interim Executive Assistant to Executive Director Nihad Awad), Ellen Barmach (Middle School Social Studies teacher at Kellman Brown Academy), Jar-El Volcy (Assistant Executive Director for the Office of Senator Sharif Street), Kevin Peréz-Allen (Deputy Director of Communications for NALEO Educational Fund), Rachel Zivic (Principal, Kellman Brown Academy), Rhonda Williams (Administrative Coordinator for the Racial Empowerment Collaborative), and Sarah Watson (ESL Teacher at KIPP Lanning Square Middle School).

There are several people whose ongoing support, generosity, and encouragement enabled me to write this book and to bring the Demystifying Diversity project from a dream to a reality.

Rayna Epstein, assistant extraordinaire, sought me out on Instagram and we immediately connected. I could tell from the instant we first spoke that she cares deeply about people. She has done everything from securing interviews and developing contacts and connections to writing show notes to reminding me to practice self-care. She is a gift in my life and I can only hope to add as much value to her life as she adds to mine.

Zack James of Rebel Hill Consulting has been a friend, a mentor, a marketing guru, a sounding board and a cheerleader from long before the inception of this project. We met years ago and have been working together since so far back I can't recall the year, but I know we met when I acted in a commercial that he was producing. We stayed in touch and, shortly thereafter, I hired him as a consultant. Zack has supported me in my career and believed in me with unwavering consistency. His hugs are priceless.

Paul Kondo, the audio engineer for the *Demystifying Diversity Podcast*, offered invaluable insight, feedback, and expertise. My dear friend Jeanette Woods was a virtual encyclopedia—a boundless resource who saved me time, money, and unnecessary energy by providing invaluable insights. Monica Lynn, a brilliant graphic designer, provided the logo, the Demystifying Diversity collage, and the podcast graphic, which the incredible Doug West adapted to create a book cover that I hope encapsulates the spirit and the synergy of this book.

Thank you to Victor Volkman, CEO of Loving Healing Press, who agreed to publish this book the second I told him about it. "The world needs this book," he told me. Victor recognized that demystifying diversity is foundational to healing from the devastating impact of discrimination. I am incredibly fortunate to have a publisher who believes in my work, respects my ideas, honors my requests, and sees me as an equal partner in the journey from pen to page to print. Victor's contributions have made this book so much better and I love working with a publisher who prioritizes people over profits.

Thank you to Kyle V. Hiller, the editor of this book. I am a huge admirer of Kyle's editing and his writing and, frankly, have been geeking out over his opinion pieces for years. It felt serendipitous when Victor let me choose my own editor for this book and Kyle was not only available but eager to take on the task and to write the forward! To have a chance to work with one of my all-time favorite contemporary authors marks the realization of a dream. Thank you, Kyle. You'll never fully know how much your involvement means to me.

A special shout-out to my co-collaborator, friend, and soul sister AnnaMarie Jones. AnnaMarie and I have laughed together, cried together, and learned together. I am thankful every day that we want to positively impact the world with our work and that we complement one another beautifully. She's always there, personally and professionally. I hope I'm as good a friend to her as she is to me.

I want to thank my sister, Tyla. She may be 12 years younger but she's a whole lot wiser. She was there throughout this journey, helping me to see my blind spots and offering insights about everything from the podcast logo and graphics to the trailer and the contents of this book. She had the courage to question my choices and tell me when my ideas lacked inspiration. My work is better because of her and I am better because of her. Even when we're not talking about this as work, Tyla and I have deep and meaningful conversations about race, religion, sexuality, diversity, and how we see ourselves within the social collective. She believes in my work and I believe in her. I can't wait to support her career as wholeheartedly as she's supported mine. When-ever I think about her as a child, I think about how our entire family used to refer to her, even then, as "the epitome of love." She is still that and it's her capacity to love people unreservedly in advance that I am trying to cultivate within myself.

I owe a debt of gratitude to the season one podcast sponsors, but since this book went to press prior to the official onboarding of all the sponsors, I'll just say a general thank you to all with a special shout-out to Next Level Trainings. I never expected when I signed up for an emotional intelligence-based leadership development training workshop that it would change my life. My friend Alexa Henderson, one of the owners of Next Level Trainings, urged me to attend and doing so opened my heart and inspired me to do this work.

Thank you to the fans of the *Demystifying Diversity Podcast* who inspire me by their willingness to listen and learn and to you, the reader, for joining me in the movement towards personal development and societal improvement. I hope to hear from you about your reactions to this book and the actions that you take as a result of reading it and engaging with the workbook, which I highly recommend purchasing to help you internalize the information presented in this book.

Last, but not least, I owe a special debt of gratitude to my mother, Sunny Taylor, who not only proofread every word of this book (except for the acknowledgements—surprise, Mom!), but also reviewed every podcast transcript, the website graphics, logo, and promotional materials, sat for an on-the-record interview, and encouraged me both with her tangible contributions of time, insights, and attention to detail, but encouraged me emotionally as well. It was my mother who taught me to embrace all aspects of myself and to care about others and connect with them as humans. My mother is my sun, my stars and my moon. Our relationship has stretched us both and hurt us both and healed us both, and I would not be the woman I am without her. This book would also not be what it is without her. Thank you Mom, and thank you everyone.

About the Author

Daralyse Lyons, aka the Transformational Storyteller, is a journalist, an actor, and an activist. She has written more than two dozen full-length books, a handful of short stories, and countless articles, performed in various plays and comedy improv shows. A member of the National Association of Black Journalists (NABJ) and a summa cum laude graduate of NYU, with a double-major in English and Religious Studies and a minor in History, she is passionate about exposing the painful side of our collective past, the side that is not written by oppressors. Through her studies, she has come to see the beautiful and overlapping philosophies of Judaism, Islam and Christianity and wonders why people so often use religion as a battering ram, instead of a source of connection and cohesion. As a Biracial woman, she has made it her mission to stand for a more integrated world. As a sexually fluid person who has had relationships and experiences with both men and women, she has had to find her place amidst a multitude of communities that attempt to erase her orientation and has been a voice within the darkness.

After writing an award-winning children's book (*I'm Mixed!* under the pseudonym Maggy Williams) about embracing her multiethnic heritage, Daralyse found her passion and her purpose educating others about the need to embrace all aspects of themselves. Since then, she has written and spoken extensively on the subject of diversity. Her perspective is one that looks to acknowledge the past while refusing to become incapacitated by it.

To connect with her directly, or to learn more, please visit www.demystifyingdiversitypodcast.com or www.daralyselyons.com

Index

W

X

Z

Level-Up Your Understanding and Compassion
with the *Demystifying Diversity Workbook* companion

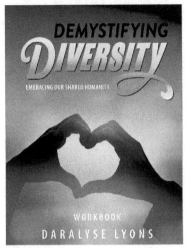

Through empathy and understanding, we can create a more inclusive world. But empathy and understanding are not purely intellectual—they require application. In the *Demystifying Diversity Workbook*, Biracial journalist Daralyse Lyons offers tangible tools for moving beyond biases and increasing one's capacity for connection. This workbook is meant to act as a companion to *Demystifying Diversity: Embracing our Shared Humanity*, in which Daralyse Lyons reveals her most important takeaways from her interviews with more than 100 individuals about a variety of topics related to diversity, equity and inclusion. Here, you are invited to go deeper, to move from awareness to action and to develop your capacity for authentic connection. It is in this space that empathy and equity become possible.

~ ~ ~

"We're Venn diagrams in Venn diagrams. And so, if you can't find those connections, it means you're not looking."
  – Alisa Kraut, assistant curator at the National Museum of American Jewish History

"Every single one of us is personally implicated in this."
                    – Cinder Kuss, liberation and social justice activist

"I don't think you can be an honest observer of the human condition without being overwhelmed at times by the cruelty that gets visited on people; this seems to be so counter to who we are. We're beautiful. Every one of us is beautiful. There is nothing like a human being in this world that we experience. We are remarkable."
                    – Dennis Moritz, poet and playwright

"*Demystifying Diversity* is an important step in our collective, arduous, complex journey towards inclusivity."
                    – Kyle V. Hiller, award winning arts & culture journalist,
                    interdisciplinary artist, author of *The Recital*

ISBN 978-1-61599-536-3

Loving Healing Press

CPSIA information can be obtained
at www.ICGtesting.com
Printed in the USA
JSHW020838121020
8534JS00012B/17